*There comes a time in every rightly constructed boys life
when he has a raging desire to go somewhere and dig for
hidden treasure.*

Mark Twain
The Adventures of Tom Sawyer

D1105085

TREASURE
IN A
CORNFIELD

TREASURE IN A CORNFIELD

THE DISCOVERY AND EXCAVATION
OF THE STEAMBOAT ARABIA

AN ADVENTURE
BY

GREG HAWLEY

PADDLE WHEEL PUBLISHING
KANSAS CITY, MO

PADDLE WHEEL PUBLISHING
Division of the Arabia Steamboat Museum
400 Grand Boulevard
Kansas City, Missouri 64106

Copyright © 1998 by Greg Hawley

All rights reserved including the right to reproduce this book or
portions thereof in any form.

Printed in Canada

Publisher's Cataloging-in-Publication Data

Hawley, Greg.
        Treasure in a cornfield : the discovery and excavation of the
    steamboat Arabia : an adventure / by Greg Hawley. -- 1st ed.
        p. cm.
        Includes bibliographical references.
        Preassigned LCCN: 97-66734
        ISBN: 0-9657612-5-8

        1. Arabia (Ship) 2. Shipwrecks--Missouri River. 3.
    Treasure-trove--Missouri River Valley. 4. Salvage--Missouri River
    Valley. 5. Steamboats--Missouri River. I. Title.

    G530.A73H39 1997   363.1'23'0978
                                        QBI97-41075

To my partners who journeyed with me
through the hardships of treasure hunting
and the thrills of discovery.

To them,
and especially to my father and mother,
Harland (Bob) and Florence Hawley,
and my wife, Karen,
and our three children, Derek, Kristin, and Megan.

ACKNOWLEDGMENTS

The author is grateful to the many individuals who contributed immeasurably to the excavation of the *Arabia*, preservation of its cargo, and museum development. To them, and especially to Norman and Beulah Sortor, for allowing us the opportunity to recover the treasures of "the Great White Arabia."

To my River Salvage partners and their wives, Harland (Bob) and Florence Hawley, Dave and Laurie Hawley, and Jerry and Joan Mackey, my thanks.

To our investors, without whose support the excavation would not have been possible, I thank Dr. Keith and Betty Broughton, Ronald and Sharon Mackey, Larry Miller, Darrel and Deanne Porter, Duane and Joyce Porterfield, Mark and Rita Hawley Scherer, and Patrica Smith.

We were greatly assisted by preservation consultants Clifford Cook and Dr. Lorne Murdock of the Historical Resource Conservation Branch of the Canadian Parks Service, Dr. David Grattan, Judith A. Logan, Carl Schlichting, and Tara Grant of the Canadian Conservation Institute.

We are grateful to Charlotte and Roger Banks, of RO-BANKS well drilling company, for helping install the dewatering wells and working at the excavation.

Many thanks to photographers Bob Hawley, Florence Hawley, Dave Hawley, Sonie Liebler, Greg Mackey, Harry Barth, Beulah Sortor, Tim Ross, and Kenneth Gates, to Kim Guerin, Elizabeth Soderberg, Ann Fondorf, and Walter Plourd for research, to Debra Shouse for editorial help, Candy Shock, Tristan Smith, Greta Rowland, Andrés Rodríguez, and Sonie Liebler for proofreading, Gary Lucy, Jim Murray, and Tony Ridder for artwork, and Dave Orf for layout and illustration work.

And finally, I am grateful to my mother, Florence Hawley, for keeping a journal of the excavation, which made writing this detailed account possible.

CONTENTS

TREASURE
IN A
CORNFIELD

FOREWORD

In Search of Treasure

With flashlights in hand, my father and I ducked out of the daylight and into the old dark goldmine. The shaft was narrow and the ceiling low. Moss-covered timbers shored up the mine and the mountain above. I jabbed my knife into a support beam, testing the wood for strength. It sliced like butter. Dad and I began whispering, fearing the vibration from noise might bring the mountain down. Ice-cold water dripped from the ceiling and ran down my neck. With one cautious step after another, we moved deep into the mine, following steel rails that once supported carts filled with precious ore. Looking behind me, the mine's opening resembled a faint star in a galaxy of blackness. Ten steps later, I turned again; the light had disappeared. The narrow tunnel twisted and turned as we journeyed into the heart of the mountain.

"The miner was following this," my father said, pointing to a vein of ore ingrained in the ceiling. "It's a small vein. Let's hope it gets larger."

Dad and I sloshed through ankle-deep water, penetrating deeper and deeper into the mine, using the vein of ore to guide us. Suddenly the vein split, and so did the mine. Shining our flashlights directly overhead, we saw a tunnel rising straight up into the mountain.

"Be careful, Greg! One misplaced step might be your last," Dad warned, as he began to scale the wall.

"I'm worried more about Mom," I said. "If she finds out we climbed up this shaft, we'll never hear the end of it."

With small rocks for hand holds, I slowly followed Dad up the shaft.

"Watch out!" he yelled, as a melon-sized stone bounced by, followed by a shower of small rocks. The large stone had narrowly missed me. Pausing to calm my nerves, I listened to the rocks crash into the shaft below. Despite the coolness of the mine, I was soon sweating. The rocks were slippery, and my hands and forearms ached from holding on by my fingertips. Each step upward was a nerve-wracking maneuver that seemed to defy gravity. I was scared of falling—it was a long way down—and I wondered if Dad was scared too. We talked little as we climbed, needing to concentrate on our footing and balance. Finally,

Dad reached up and placed his hand on the ceiling of the shaft.

"Hold my light," Dad instructed, as he reached for his rock hammer and ore sack with his free hand. With his legs braced on a small ledge, Dad hammered away at rocks with promising color. Suddenly, one of the flashlights I held went dark.

"Dad," I whispered, "my light stopped working."

"It's a good thing we brought two lights," he said. The words barely left his mouth when the second light quit. Darkness swallowed us instantly. I could not get either light to come on.

"What now?" I said, trying to disguise my fear.

"Well, we can't go up, that's for sure," Dad replied.

Climbing the vertical shaft with lights had been difficult. Descending in total blackness seemed hopeless. I was slightly below my father, so I had to move first. Lifting my right foot, I nervously lowered my leg over the edge. Finding a toehold by sense of touch, I shoved my boot into the crevice and applied some weight. At first the foothold seemed solid, but as I shifted more weight to my right leg, the ledge moved and suddenly broke away. I hung on by my fingernails as rocks tumbled and crashed into the main shaft. My hands were shaking as I lowered my foot again. I found a solid ledge and inched my way down the rock wall. Dad was directly above me. Every three feet I stopped to wait for him. I reached up with one hand, felt for his feet and blindly guided them, one at a time, into cracks or onto ledges. I paused occasionally to drop a rock, then counted the seconds before the rock hit to see how far above the main shaft we remained. When we finally reached the lower shaft, I felt an overwhelming sense of relief. Unfortunately, we were not yet out of the mine.

Night is dark, but not as dark as a goldmine. I closed my eyes to see if there was any difference. There was none. We saw by sense of touch. Inch by inch, Dad and I felt our way through the shaft. It seemed that hours passed before a ray of light pierced the darkness. The proverbial "light at the end of the tunnel" suddenly had a special meaning for me.

Emerging from the goldmine, I took a deep breath of Colorado air. The sun's warmth felt good on my cold face, and the adrenaline that had flooded my veins subsided. I felt invigorated at having survived the darkness of the mine.

Dad looked at his watch as he climbed into the jeep and declared, "We have just enough time to drive to town and get two more lights."

After searching for gold deep in the mountain, Greg and his father emerge from the mine.
Photo by Karen Hawley

Bob Hawley explores a narrow shaft that miners abandoned long ago.
Photo by Florence Hawley

Bob Hawley inspects the vertical shaft before starting the climb.   Photo by Greg Hawley

It is my hope this story
will ignite within you a spark of adventure;
for me, the memories will sustain
and entertain me when I am no longer able
to walk the river's edge.

CHAPTER 1

Treasure Along the River

Treasure hunting has always been a part of my life. From digging in goldmines high in the Rocky Mountains to exploring the banks of the Missouri River, I lived my childhood searching for treasure.

The river was always a backyard playground in my home town of Independence, Missouri. I spent many hours with my childhood companions fishing deep pools cut from the channel by the Missouri's mighty current. My friends and I sat patiently on the sandbars and stretched fish stories into unbelievable lies. We watched the fishing line where it entered the water, waiting and hoping that the fish of a lifetime would take the bait.

As the cool air of autumn replaced the hot breathless days of summer, hunting replaced fishing, although we did not require the presence of game. The leaves of the giant sycamores that lined the riverbanks wilted to seasonal changes and fell to the river below. This colorful blanket of fall tapestry, combined with sticks and logs, floated slowly downriver. They created an endless parade of moving targets and provided our imaginations with ample dragons to slay.

With the passing of winter, spring rains transformed the river into a boiling quagmire of mud, water, and debris. Receding waters deposited unwanted clutter for countless miles along its banks.

For my friends and me, the riverbank debris was an endless highway of undiscovered treasure, stretching as far as our bravery and bony legs of youth could carry us. Tramping along the river, we played with discarded bottles and balls, fishing lures, and furniture. We defeated Indians at the river's first bend and monsters at the next. This playground at the river's edge was a separate world; it was ours to conquer.

As an adult, my family, friends, and I continued to hunt treasure along the banks of the Missouri. One day in 1985, I received a call.

"Let's meet for lunch and discuss buried treasure." My father's voice rang loud and clear over the two-way radio in my truck.

"Repeat that, please. Did you say buried treasure?" I asked.

Only a static hiss replied—he had signed off.

In the hot months of summer, business consumed all the hours of daylight. So it surprised me to hear Dad mention anything that wasn't business related. From the briefness of his statement, I knew he was serious.

At the age of 27, I found myself firmly entrenched as a husband, father of two children, and blue-collar worker attempting to make ends meet. In our small family refrigeration business, my mother, Florence, answered the phone and kept the books; my older brother, Dave, and I ran residential and commercial service calls; and my father orchestrated the entire schedule and oversaw business operations. My older sister, Rita, also helped with the business, but her primary interest and career was in music. As a child, I began learning the business by carrying my father's tool pouch for five cents a service call. My father taught me in the field and constantly discussed business around the family dinner table. I seemed destined to follow in his footsteps and become an air-conditioning and refrigeration repairman.

At Hi-Boy, our traditional eating place, I found my father, Bob, brother, Dave, and Jerry Mackey, operator of the restaurant, talking intently in the corner booth.

My father and Jerry were friends from way back. Dad met Jerry through working on refrigeration equipment at the restaurant. Both men had come from humble beginnings and succeeded in building their own businesses. Their mutual admiration and respect had developed into a deep friendship. Each possessed incredible work ethics and attributes that demonstrated a love for God, family, and community.

Dave, like the rest of our family, was an adventurer. Spending time outdoors, prowling through goldmines, and searching for ghost towns were a common pastime for my brother.

"You guys must have gotten your work done early today," I said, as I approached the table. They were talking so intently they hardly noticed me. If they leaned in any closer across the table their heads would bump.

"What's the big secret?" I asked, toning my voice down to a whisper and sliding in beside them.

Dave began retelling a story he had heard about sunken steamboats on the Missouri River. During an air-conditioning service call, the home owner claimed that several steamers sank during the 1800s, and their oaken hulls and cargo remained hidden in the river valley.

Our discussion intensified as we talked of steamboats and hidden treasure. The river's course had changed dramatically since the 1800s. If boats containing gold, silver, or valuable cargo did sink, then some likely remained buried under dry land in the old river channel.

We decided to seek more information on sunken steamers. That brief meeting marked the beginning of a life-altering adventure. Four naive treasure hunters, along with our families, began a quest that would span many years. That lunch began a search for the mother lode, not in goldmines, but beneath corn and bean fields in the Missouri River Valley.

Research and Exploration

For the third time in less than an hour, the librarian looked up from her desk and glared at us over her reading glasses. She gave my partners and me a look that only a librarian can. "Sssshhh, be quiet." Being quiet is difficult when researching buried treasure. Discovering an article referring to gold or silver lost aboard a sunken steamer is cause to burst out with chatter well above library limits.

Each of us spent time doing research at libraries and courthouses throughout the Midwest, and Dave even traveled to Washington, D.C., and looked through the national archives.

Whenever there was a free moment, I stepped out of my service truck and into a public library. My dirty blue jeans, flannel shirt, and worn leather work boots drew almost everyone's attention. I looked out of place, but didn't care. Libraries housed dusty old books with yellowing pages that held clues to the whereabouts of lost steamboats.

The history books verified that steamboats had sunk in the Missouri River, and in numbers much larger than we expected. Some estimates placed the numbers of sunken steamers at 400; although official reports from Captain H. M. Chittenden, U.S. Army Corps of Engineers, showed the total as 289. Due to the length of the river, we centered our research on steamers lost in Missouri, Kansas, southern Nebraska, and Iowa, all within a one-day drive.

Although books provided valuable background information on steamboats and their role during the Westward expansion movement, nineteenth-century river community newspapers provided more detailed accounts. News of a sunken steamer spread quickly. Other steamboats passing by the wreck carried the unfortunate story upstream and downstream to a variety of newspapers. Our eyes strained from the glare of microfilm machines as we scanned the papers for bold headings that gave clues of disaster: LIVES LOST, BOILER EXPLOSION, STEAMER SUNK, SERIOUS ACCIDENT.

As stories of steamboats unfolded, their history and significance became increasingly apparent. Thirteen years after the Lewis and Clark expedition, the first steamboat *Independence* ventured upstream. The small steamer's destination was Franklin and Chariton, both thriving communities on the lower Missouri. Leaving St. Louis on May 17, 1819, the *Independence*, captained by John Nelson, embarked on a historic journey with a cargo of flour, sugar, whiskey, and iron castings.

The *Independence* blazed a pathway that others would soon follow. Many cumbersome deep-hulled steamers, while native to the Mississippi River, floundered attempting the shallows of the Missouri. The failure of these large and unwieldy steamboats sparked design alterations that eventually led to lightly built, flat-bottom boats. Fully loaded, these new steamers floated in a mere four feet of water. The structural and mechanical evolution of the Missouri steamboat turned the once impassable Missouri into one of the world's great carriers of commerce.

These advancements gave birth to the Golden Age of steamboating. During the decade of 1850 to 1860, a person could not stand on the bank of the Old Muddy without seeing a steamboat either coming or going. The cry of "Steamboat-a-comin'!" echoed daily through the streets of river communities.

With river traffic on the increase, the rate of steamboat fatalities rose dramatically. Fires, boiler explosions, and high winds consumed many steamers, while floating ice cut down others. However, these catastrophes, though frequent, could not compare with the destruction wrought by hidden tree snags.

The meandering course of the river undercut thousands of sycamores, oaks, and walnut trees, tipping them into the current. As a tree drifted downstream, the less buoyant root system eventually became mired in the muddy river bottom. The main trunk and upper canopy would swing with the force of the current until it pointed downstream. Over time, the strong current, combined with floating debris such as ice and logs, tore all but the most sturdy limbs from the trunk. The result of nature's work was a menacing battering ram facing downstream. Steamers unfortunate enough to plow head-on into these hidden obstacles found themselves hopelessly sinking to the river's bottom or at the very least crippled. Seventy percent of all steamboats on the Missouri sank due to snags. So torturous was the river that the estimated life expectancy of a Missouri steamboat was only five years.

An experienced pilot was the best defense against these formidable opponents. Pilots could detect submerged snags by "ripples" or "breaks" in the water, though the sun's reflection on the river helped camouflage the snags. Strong winds also disturbed the river's surface, making it difficult to see changes in the muddy water.

The meandering current of the Old Muddy greatly complicated navigation. Not only did the river's constant alteration create thousands of dangerous obstacles, but the changing course made memorization of the channel nearly impossible. Pilots took great pride in their acquired knowledge of the river. They memorized obstructions while traveling upstream so they could safely pass them on the return.

"In order to be a pilot a man had to learn more than any man ought to be allowed to know," Mark Twain wrote in *Life on the Mississippi*. Describing the requirements of a riverboat pilot, he added: "He must learn it all over again in a different way every 24 hours."

The completion of the railroad during the late 1800s pushed the American steamboat into oblivion. Like skeletons of giant dinosaurs, sunken steamboats rest undisturbed, deep within the grave of the Missouri River basin. Due to the meandering course of the Missouri River, many of these forgotten steamers are no longer beneath the river. Rich farmland now cradles them.

Like the steamboats, the river too has changed. To improve river travel, the U.S. Army Corps of Engineers has harnessed the river. Pilings, cable, and rock stretch into the river controlling its flow, and levees parallel its banks to restrict wandering. No more does she stretch from bluff to bluff, her current gracefully spreading across countless miles of marshland. She is no longer responsible for breeding poem and song, nor the creation and destruction of heroes and villains.

As we searched for lost steamers containing great wealth, we were mesmerized by other stories printed in old newspapers. Life along the river was boiling with dangerous adventure: bear attacks, duels to the death, run away slaves, Indians attacking and being attacked. Learning about these early river days ranked second in importance to our quest for buried treasure, but just barely.

"You guys need to move your stuff into the other room," Mom said in a stern tone. My partners and I were having a meeting; and river maps, pencils, rulers, and stacks of research material covered up Mom's kitchen table, and she wanted it back.

After reviewing our findings, my partners and I decided to search for several steamboats. Each boat held great potential. Some we believed contained gold and silver, while others were attractive for their precious cargo of merchandise. We were most interested in the steamboats *Mollie Dozzier*, *E.A. Ogden*, *Twilight*, *Mars*, *William Baird*, *Arabia*, *Princess*, *George Washington*, *Radnor*, and a nameless boat that sank near Boonville, Missouri. To investigate and find all 400 steamboats that sank into the Missouri River would take a lifetime. Sitting around Mom's kitchen table, we decided to begin the second phase of our treasure hunt. It was time to find, evaluate, and choose at least one steamboat to excavate.

Classic novels like Robert Louis Stevenson's *Treasure Island* conjure up images of a parrot perched on the shoulder of a villainous, one-legged captain, sword-waving pirates, skull and cross bones, and a map where X marks the treasure. Modern treasure hunting is very different. Rather than taking a shipful of pirates to an uncharted island and charging through the jungle with sabers drawn, we simply walked up to a landowner's house, knocked on the door, and said, "Hello, we'd like to look for a steamboat underneath your cornfield." In most cases, their first reaction was an expression that said, "What nut house did you come from?" But once we showed them our research and shared the excitement over the possibility of finding buried treasure, most farmers consented.

One of the first boats we looked for was a mysterious steamboat that had sunk above Franklin, Missouri, in the summer of 1819. Legend and fact suggest that this early steamer was part of the famed Yellowstone Expedition, led by Major Stephen H. Long. Although the dates, names, and cargo amounts vary depending on the source, the following news article from the *Boonville Weekly Eagle*, dated October 8, 1875, represents a small portion of research material accumulated on this legendary steamboat:

Buried Treasure
$200,000 in the Missouri River

Mr. W. L. Scott of this city, who was one of the earliest settlers of this section of county, and a perfectly reliable man, has given us the following for publication: In July, 1819, the second steamboat that ever passed up the Missouri struck a snag at the head of Hardeman's Island, between Boonville and Arrow Rock, and immediately sunk. The boat was loaded principally with government stores. It had in the hold a large quantity of Kentucky whiskey, and also $200,000 in silver coin, which was being taken to Council Bluffs to pay the government troops stationed at that place, which was the extreme outpost of civilization. Mr. Scott, though a small boy at the time, lived very near the scene of the accident, and remembers well what was related by the officers of the boat at the time, looking after the lost treasure. When the government agents arrived, the river had swollen to such an extent that no vestige of the boat was to be seen, and they reported to the government that it was impossible to recover the money, or any portion of the cargo.

Fifty-six years have passed, yet Mr. Scott says he can now point out the exact place where the unfortunate steamer lies buried with its valuable cargo. He is probably the only man living who can do so, and he is well advanced in years. The government can yet reclaim the money if it will make the effort; or, if a release can be given by the government, private parties will undoubtedly undertake it.

Based on our research, the area in which the steamer sank could easily stretch over several square miles of farmland or rest beneath the present river channel.

Once we gained permission from landowners, we combed the land with a magnetometer, which indicates the presence of ferrous metal hidden within the earth. This state-of-the-art equipment measures electromagnetic fields of the earth. Any large metal structures disrupting the magnetic field consistency are registered upon the magnetometer's light-emitting diode (L.E.D.) readout screen.

I thought it would be easy to traverse the flat farmland with the six-pound magnetometer in hand. Reality was another matter altogether. The challenges of exploration varied drastically with the seasonal changes prevalent in the Midwest. Planted crops that stretched skyward made a summer search difficult. Crops of soybeans three feet tall tangled about our legs and made keeping our balance nearly impossible. Fields of corn, some exceeding a mile in length, swallowed us whole. Walking submerged in this sea of green, the razor-edged leaves slashed at our faces and arms, and sweat burned the lacerations.

Our hopes soared with each signal registered upon our magnetometer. Our first big signal captured the imagination of everyone. Even the skeptical farmer joined in and offered the use of his backhoe. For over two hours we dug in the soft sand. When the backhoe raked across wood at a depth of 12 feet, images of sparkling treasure filled my mind. We gathered around the hole like anxious children, but our discovery was not a steamer filled with gold. Instead, we had uncovered a cluster of timbers wrapped in steel cable. It was a flood control structure left over from work done by the Corps of Engineers years earlier. Disappointment hung in the air, and our hopes collapsed as quickly as they had soared.

The wet bottomland along the Missouri holds claim to some of the most impenetrable swamps and thickets in the country. An endless supply of groundwater, combined with peak humidity, created an entanglement of vegetation that was nearly impassable. The swamps seemed bottomless when we attempted to cross on foot. We dared not stop or we would sink in a quagmire of mud. Adding to this, the terrain was the ultimate breeding ground for pesky mosquitoes and biting horseflies. Wading through waist-high water and crawling through thickets with magnetometers in hand left us with respectful memories of summer exploration.

After harvest, we used the rows of bean and corn stubble to guide us. If the ground was dry and we started walking at first light, we could cover one square mile by dark. Unfortunately, October rains soon transformed the dusty fields into a sticky mess. The water-soaked topsoil clung to our boots with unyielding strength. Each step was a lesson in frustration as the mud accumulated in weight. To shed the heavy earth, we kicked at what must have appeared an imaginary foe, sending mud flying. Then we stepped out again, only to have our efforts and strength neutralized by the mud's stockpiling weight.

We continued our search into the winter, battling freezing rain, snow, and relentless northern winds. Wind chills dropped to 30 degrees below zero, and our numb fingers made operating the magnetometer difficult. The silver lining of this cloud of sub-zero misery was that the bitter cold froze the ground making walking easy.

Magnetometers are extremely sensitive. Every acre indicated the presence of metal hidden beneath the ground surface. Not knowing how a steamboat would register upon our magnetometer, we investigated each signal, using drills with core-sampling ability, backhoes, steel probes, old-fashioned hand shoveling, and innovative water jets to pierce the earth.

Bob Hawley searches for steamboats with a magnetometer. Walking ten miles a day across difficult terrain was not uncommon.

Photo by Greg Hawley

On one occasion, a strong reading upon the magnetometer indicated the presence of a large metal structure deep beneath us. We positioned a backhoe over the area and began digging. When the backhoe struck what appeared to be large timbers with iron attached, Jerry Mackey and I slid into the 12-foot deep trench and began scooping away sand.

"This has got to be the boat," I said, as we dug away sand from the timbers.

"We'll soon find out," Jerry said, smiling despite the mud covering his face.

"Can you tell what it is?" Dave asked.

"I bet it's a boat," Dad said in a wishful tone.

Consumed with excitement, Jerry and I continued to shovel away sand. Suddenly, as if someone called out our names, Jerry and I stopped digging and looked at one another. Terror gripped my throat.

"Get out of the hole!" Jerry shouted. His words mirrored the panic surging through my body. The deep trench was about to cave-in. Jerry scrambled up the embankment, fighting the wet sandy soil. Clawing his way to the top, he turned and reached down for me. As I grasped his hand, I felt the earth collapsing around me. Jerry dragged me to solid ground just in time. When I stopped shaking, I stared at what had almost been my grave. The cave-in had instantly filled the hole. The excitement of treasure hunting had interfered with good judgment.

"Don't tell your mother," Dad said. Our brush with death left us momentarily weak in the knees, but stronger in our appreciation of life.

Using the backhoe to widen the hole, we discovered there was no boat, but instead iron supports, steel cable, and timbers from previous Corps of Engineers work.

Jerry and I rode home together that evening and discussed the near tragic event. We both agreed; it was our decision to climb in and dig, but the notion to climb out quickly came from a much greater power.

Every night, I returned home physically exhausted and mentally frustrated. My wife, Karen, no longer asked if we had found anything. A simple glance into my eyes told the story. Throughout the quest, Karen never discouraged my efforts. A love affair with a steamboat had taken her man away, but she remained supportive.

"Drive carefully," Karen said, "and this time, try to be home for dinner."

Waving good-bye to my wife had become a ritual. I could not remember the last time I had spent a Saturday at home with my family. Searching for lost steamboats required a huge amount of time, although working to pay bills and feeding the family remained our first priority. Our family business was seasonal. When work slowed, I often did all the service calls and my brother and father searched for steamboats. Other times, my father or brother shouldered the work load and allowed the other two to explore. We spent entire weekends at the river. Balancing treasure hunting, family, and Sunday church services was challenging for all the partners.

Over miles of fields, thickets, and swamps, we searched for the elusive wreck of 1819. We made many discoveries, but farm machinery, rolls of steel cable, car parts, steel fence posts, and a street sign did not satisfy us. The reality of steamboat hunting began to sink in. After months of work, we reluctantly concluded this steamboat was not under dry land, but somewhere beneath the river.

It was time to pursue a new quarry.

The *George Washington* sank in 1826 and the *Radnor* in 1846. Both steamers hit tree snags and sank in the same region. The *George Washington* carried government supplies consisting of food, firearms, and a gold shipment to pay troops. The *Radnor* carried general supplies for frontier communities.

Our search for these vessels continued with enthusiasm. But after months of searching, the results were negative. Both steamers either remained beneath the river, or the river's current had broken them apart and scattered them downriver.

Our research indicated the *Mars* carried a cargo of general merchandise when it sank at Cogswell Landing on July 8, 1865. Historical information seemed accurate, and finding this boat appeared certain. We made a contractual agreement with the landowner and eagerly began the search. We detected a huge signal and felt confident it was the *Mars*. However, oil refineries had installed pipe lines directly through the search area. The risk of damaging the pipe line through extensive core sampling or excavating was too high. We abandoned the *Mars*.

Less than a mile downriver, near Napoleon, Missouri, the steamboat *Princess* sank on July 1, 1868. Its cargo consisted of supplies for Fort Benton, Montana. The entire search area was a dense thicket. After several days of crawling through or under heavy vegetation, the only discovery that resembled a boat was the hull of a steel tugboat that sank in the 1960s.

The largest boat on our list was the *E.A. Ogden*. Sinking in February 1860, its cargo consisted of military supplies and a gold shipment for Fort Leavenworth. It measured 280 feet in length and carried 400 tons of freight. Its location was six miles above Jefferson City. After several days of looking, a massive signal registered on our equipment. With the use of probe rods we confirmed the location. Unfortunately, a portion of the steamer was under the river. Excavating a steamboat from the Missouri River was possible, but also expensive. We decided to leave the *E.A. Ogden* behind.

The *Mollie Dozzier* came next. With a boat load of 245 miners coming from the Montana gold fields, and a million dollars in gold, the steamer hit a tree and sank on October 1, 1866. Lost near the town of Chamois, Missouri, several miners weighted down by leather money belts drowned. For months after, survivors of the wreck camped along the riverbank, hoping to recover the bodies and gold.

The steamer rests in a swamp named Mollie Dozzier Chute. With the use of maps and a magnetometer, Dave waded through the swamp and found the boat easily. A million dollars in gold at 1866 prices is a staggering amount at today's value. But there was one problem. Prior to core sampling the steamer, we found a different newspaper with conflicting information. This paper stated the *Mollie Dozzier* struck a snag and sank for the first time in Nebraska. According to the article, the crew unloaded all the cargo, repaired the hole, and floated the boat. Deck hands began reloading the freight back on the steamer, but the miners refused to go aboard with their gold. They claimed the *Mollie Dozzier* was too weak for their precious cargo and took passage on a different steamer. Which article was correct? The answer is still beneath the mud in the Mollie Dozzier Chute.

The *William Baird* was also a promising boat. It struck a snag and sank opposite Waverly, Missouri, in 1858, while carrying 150 passengers, $5,000 in gold, and whiskey.

Complicating our search was the steamboat *Tropic*. It sank in the same area, and determining which boat was which presented a concern. Because the *Tropic* sank on her downriver trip, her cargo likely consisted of grain, hemp, and other worthless freight.

The first day searching for the *Willaim Baird*, my father received a significant signal on the magnetometer. Using an air-powered drill with a three-inch diameter bit, we tested the site. The drill moved easily through the sand, then began shaking violently at a depth of 35 feet. With a confirmed hit, I felt like a kid with a giant fish on the end of the line.

"Do you think it's a boat?" I asked, looking for encouragement.

"Might be," Jerry replied. "But it could be just an old tree."

Holding the drill steady, we allowed the corkscrew action of the bit to lift debris to the surface. After two minutes of anxious waiting, pieces of wood boiled to the top. Still uncertain, we moved and repeated the process. As I watched the drill disappear into the earth for the second time, I thought of my wife. If I could just tell her we found a steamboat that held promise, it would make things a little easier around the house. Five minutes later the bit shook violently, confirming a hit. It was like playing the game pin the tail on the donkey, sometimes hitting, other times missing. The size and configuration confirmed we had indeed found a steamboat. Unfortunately, it was not the right one. Official government records showed the *William Baird* and the *Tropic* as much longer boats. The identity of this uncharted steamer may never be known.

A few days later, I returned to the farm field. My search began along the tree-lined riverbank. I had only walked a mile when an unmistakable signal registered on the magnetometer. I was standing on a steamboat, but which one: the *Tropic* or the *William Baird*? Completing the search along the river, I began to crisscross the open fields. After walking a full four miles the magnetometer confirmed another find. Previous research describing where the steamer sank authenticated I had found the *William Baird*.

The following weekend we brought drilling equipment to the site and began outlining the steamer. The boat took shape quickly, but again there was a problem. The stern of the *William Baird* lay under a Corps of Engineers' levee. We core sampled the forward end and discovered fragments of dishes, a porcelain doll, a fish hook, broken marble furniture, and a large number of iron chains. The boat appeared laden with cargo—just the confirmation we were looking for. This was a great boat, but the Corps of Engineers wanted $100,000 to move the levee

left *Using a bucket drill, core samples are taken from the steamboat William Baird.*

Photo by Bob Hawley

right *Three generations of Hawley's dig through core samples from the steamboat William Baird. L to R: Greg, Florence, Karen, Matt, Jenny, Derek, Laurie, and Kristin.*

Photo by Dave Hawley

and replace it after the excavation. Moving and replacing the levee on our limited budget made excavating the *William Baird* impossible. Discouraged, but still hopeful, it was time to look for another steamboat.

The *Twilight* struck a snag and sank in 1865, just east of Missouri City. The boat contained a large cargo of gin, firearms, uniforms for troops, and a valuable freight of general supplies. Salvagers attempted to recover the cargo in 1895, but records showed that these early treasure hunters recovered little.

When the *Twilight* sank, her cargo was large, and the potential value excited us. Because of the earlier salvage attempt, locating the boat was easy. I was more nervous than usual as the drill bit spun into the earth. Our list of boats was getting shorter, and we needed some good news to take home. The drill shook violently as it churned into the steamer. We crowded around as the first sample ascended and was unloaded on the ground. Digging through the muck with bare hands and shovels, our hopes quickly turned into a moment of mourning. The sample only contained black oak from the steamer's hull.

"I can't believe it," Dave said. "The *Twilight* should be full of cargo."

We drilled into the steamer four more times, but the only artifact we discovered was a brass label from a sardine can. Either the river broke the *Twilight* apart after sinking or the salvage of 1895 was more successful than we imagined.

After three years of exploring, only one steamer remained on our list: "the Great White Arabia" (as it was historically referred to).

The Great White
Arabia

The legend of the Great White *Arabia* began in 1853, in Brownsville, Pennsylvania, at the Pringle Boat-Building Company. Located on the banks of the Monongahela River, the Pringle boatyard built steamboats for clients as far away as California and South America.

John Snyder Pringle built the steamboat Arabia *in 1853 at his boatyard in Brownsville, Pennsylvania.*   Courtesy of Ann Fondorf

The Great White Arabia *weighed over 400 tons when fully loaded, but could float in a mere four feet, six inches of water.*   Illustration by Gary Lucy

The *Arabia* was an average size boat for western rivers. Measuring 171 feet in length and 54 feet in width, the steamer had a 220-ton cargo capacity. The *Arabia* traveled on both the Ohio and Mississippi rivers; then in 1855 it began serving towns on the Missouri River.

Rivermen have said for years that "a steamboat built properly can float on a head of beer, or on the sands of Arabia." On October 30, 1855, the *Missouri Daily Democrat* reported: "River so low that navigation of Missouri not occurring." Two days later: "For the Missouri - the fine steamer *Arabia*, Capt. Shaw, will leave today for Brunswick and way places...."

In its short life on the Missouri, the *Arabia* made numerous trips upriver. From St. Louis, the steamer traveled deep into Indian territory, as far as Pierre, South Dakota. The destinations varied as did the passengers. Soldiers, Mormon immigrants, gun-smuggling abolitionists, businessmen, and common travelers all used the *Arabia* as a lifeline to the West.

After traveling aboard the *Arabia,* George W. Withers, editor of the Richfield Enterprise, wrote on May 25th, 1855:

> Persons desiring to take a trip per steamer upon the Missouri River, either up or down would do well to meet the *Arabia*. We would strongly recommend her for speed and comfort. The table is supplied with all the luxuries desired and everything fixed up in a most elegant style. We were on this boat two weeks and became acquainted with all the officers and most of the crew; and assure you that the person and property of passengers is perfectly safe on board.

Merchants dependent on supplies relied heavily on the *Arabia*. Pioneers facing the long months of winter traveled many miles to stock up on goods delivered by the steamer. In an article appearing in the *Squatter Sovereign*, from Atchison, Kansas, on November 27, 1855, a merchant reported the following:

The Last Arrival

> We have just received, per steamer *Arabia* and Lewis Burnes, our Fall Stock of Assorted Merchandise, Embracing almost every article in the line of dry goods, groceries, hardware, queensware, hats, caps, boots, shoes, clothing, &c., &c. Which added to our former stock, renders our assortment more general than that of any house in the place. All which will be sold extremely low for cash only. L. Burnes & Bro's Atchison, Nov. 13, '55.

On August 30, 1856, the Great White *Arabia* steamed away from St. Louis, Missouri, and up the Missouri River, for the last time. The day of her departure, the St. Louis *Missouri Republican* wrote: "The Steamer *Arabia*, Capt. Terrill will leave for all points on the Missouri between St.

Joseph and Sioux City today at 4:00 P.M. Mr. Boyd is clerk on the *Arabia*. Passengers will find everything to their liking on board."

Carrying 130 passengers, their personal belongings, and 200 tons of new merchandise, the *Arabia* reached the City of Kansas (present-day Kansas City) in seven days. On September 5, 1856, after unloading some freight at Westport Landing, the *Arabia* puffed its way upriver in the late afternoon. As it neared Parkville, Missouri, the *Arabia* slammed into a walnut tree lying just beneath the river's surface. The tree ripped through the three-inch thick oak hull, penetrating a full ten feet, and scattering cargo in all directions. Within seconds, the boat tilted to the larboard (left) side, and water flooded the main deck.

A 1954 issue of *True Magazine* printed passenger Able D. Kirk's account of the *Arabia* sinking:

> I had just been married near Peoria, Illinois, and was on my way to Nebraska with my bride ... We embarked on the boat in St. Louis and had been on the water about ten days. The boat was heavily loaded with freight but did not have a large number of passengers. One evening when many of the passengers were at supper the boat struck a snag. We felt the shock and at once the boat started sinking. There was a wild scene on board. The boat went down till the water came over the deck, and the boat keeled over on one side. The chairs and stools were tumbled about and many of the children nearly fell into the water. Several of the men on board seized the life boat and started for the shore, but they came back and the women and children were put in the boat. They called for a small man to go with the boat and I was small and I got aboard. The river bank at the point where we landed had been caving off and was very steep. I climbed out and pulled the women ashore. Horses and wagons came down from Parkville and took us to the hotel there that night. Many of the trunks and valises were taken off the boat and stacked up in the woods near the river. That night they were broken open by thieves, and all the valuables were taken out. We were taken on the steamboat, James A.

On September 5, 1856, the steamboat Arabia, *laden with frontier supplies, struck a submerged tree and sank. The passengers saved themselves, but the steamboat and the precious cargo were lost to the Missouri River.*   **Painting by Tony Ridder**

Lucus, and when we went aboard, all that could be seen of our boat was the top of the pilot house. That sank out of sight in a short time.

In another account, dated September 19, 1856, the *Liberty Weekly Tribune* reported the sinking of the *Arabia*:

Serious Accident and Heavy Loss - On last Friday night just before night fall, the Missouri River Passenger Steamer Arabia, while in sight and nearing our city, struck a snag, which penetrated her hull in so serious a manner; that she sunk in the short space of ten minutes in twelve feet of water. No lives were lost, but the boat and cargo which was a very large one bound for points above and Council Bluffs, is a total loss. We do not know whether the Insurance Companies will attempt to recover her cargo or not; it would seem to be a hopeless task, as the water is now running over her hurricane deck in one or two places where the vessel has broken in two.

The sinking of the *Arabia* was tragic news with far-reaching ramifications. Settlers faced a hard winter without their necessary goods. Merchants suffered financial losses without the food, winter clothing, and hardware to stock shelves. Insurance companies spent thousands of dollars repaying merchants for lost freight and the owners of the *Arabia* for a portion of the boat. The officers and crew of the steamer lost their wages, while the *Arabia*'s passengers had lost their belongings to the river or to thieves.

When the *Arabia* sank into the Missouri, several insurance companies considered their policy amounts a private matter, but the St. Louis *Missouri Republican*, dated September 10, 1856, did obtain loss totals from the following companies:

> **On Hull** – America Insurance Co. $4,000
> Merchants' Co. $4,000
> **On Cargo** – Floating Dock $8,000
> St. Louis .... about $400
> Lumbermen & Merchants $1,800
> Total $18,200

On September 11, 1856, the *Daily Missouri Democrat* printed a graphic account of the *Arabia* sinking and the passengers that feared for their lives:

> *ARABIA* – The officers of this boat, which was lost in the Missouri last Friday, arrived yesterday on the Tatum. From them we learn that the sinking was a very sudden affair. The snag struck her forward of the boilers, pierced its way into the center of a lot of freight and lifted the deck several inches above its proper level. As soon as the boat was brought again under control, she was headed for the bank, but sank when she was about the distance of her own length from it. Two minutes only elapsed from the striking until she sunk. Of course the alarm and confusion

which always attends the like sudden disasters, prevailed here, but the fears of the passengers were allayed by the presence of mind displayed by her officers. We are glad to know that the only life lost on this unfortunate occasion was that of a mule, which would have been saved but for its own obstinacy.

It is really a matter to be wondered at, how quickly boats which sink in the Missouri, disappear as a general thing. When the men left this boat, on Sunday morning, the water had reached her hurricane deck, on the starboard side, and it is supposed she will now be entirely out of sight. The river is not rising, but the boat is sinking in the sand.

Some said when the steamer sank, 400 barrels of Kentucky's finest Bourbon Whiskey went with her. This liquid treasure made the *Arabia* a legend. In local taverns, barber shops, and at aristocratic events, treasure hunters and dreamers spun magical tales of the unforgettable Great White *Arabia*.

After the sinking, the course of the Missouri River slowly moved northeast, leaving the *Arabia* beneath a farm in Wyandotte County, Kansas. Although under dry land, the *Arabia* remained in water. The water table, or aquifer, stretches between the bluffs. Seasonal rainfall and river levels determine its depth, but in normal years it flows approximately six to eight feet below ground level. The presence of water gives river sand a fluid nature which makes digging difficult.

The 400 barrels of whiskey lost aboard the *Arabia* prompted several unsuccessful salvage attempts. In 1877, Robert Treadway and Henry Tobener of Kansas City used a wooden coffer dam in their attempt to reach the *Arabia*. Four months later, and at the expense of $2,000, they abandoned the dig having retrieved only one case of felt hats.

In 1897, Gale "Dad" Henson of Holt, Missouri, constructed a long steel caisson six-feet in diameter. Pressurizing the caisson with air, salvagers forced the water down and out, allowing workers to remove the sand from within the enclosed chamber. After three successful probes into the *Arabia*, Henson's team found no whiskey and stopped digging.

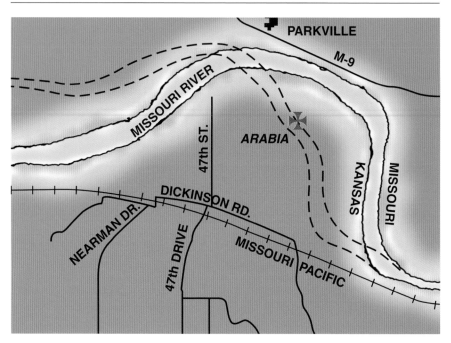

The center of the Missouri River is the border between the states. The Arabia *sank in the state of Missouri, but erosion caused the river to move north and east, eventually leaving the steamboat in the state of Kansas.*   **Illustration by Dave Orf**

The most recent salvage was in 1975. Jessie Pursell and Sam Corbino attempted the first fully open excavation of the *Arabia*. After spending several weeks and thousands of dollars pumping out water, they abandoned the effort without seeing any portion of the steamboat.

"Norman Sortor," whose family owned the land where the steamer lay hidden, "will never let anyone try for the *Arabia* again," people associated with the 1975 salvage told us. "He's tired of people digging holes and messing up the farm. Don't waste your time asking permission."

Three generations of Sortors watched salvage attempts fail. Seeing treasure hunters walk away defeated was not a new experience for the Sortor family; they expected it.

By trade, Norman Sortor was a magistrate judge and carried a reputation for being fair, yet having little patience for lawbreakers. So I was nervous when I finally mustered up the courage to call Judge Sortor. Our hopes of digging a boat now rested with the *Arabia*, but his strict reputation was intimidating. I could only hope that he would give us a chance.

When I finally made the call, I found Norman surprisingly friendly. He invited Dave and me over to chat. Norman's wife, Beulah, met us at the door and invited us in. Sitting around their dining room table, Norman showed us news clippings from previous salvage attempts.

Norman asked plenty of questions: "Do you boys have children? What do you do for a living? Where did you grow up?"

As Dave and I prepared to leave, Norman gave us some advice. "I'd rather you boys forget digging the *Arabia*. A lot of folks have tried, but all have failed; and I'd hate to see you spend a lot of money for nothing."

Despite Norman's lack of encouragement, negotiations continued. Norman met Dad and Jerry; and, after several meetings, Norman finally gave us his consent. Dave began working out terms of the agreement,

Two days of precision drilling revealed the Arabia's *configuration. Found beneath a Kansas cornfield, the* Arabia *measures 171 feet in length. Comparing the steamer's outline to the adjacent semi truck gives a perspective to the magnitude of the* Arabia.   **Photo by Dave Hawley**

and after nearly a year Norman signed on the dotted line. The contractual terms stated that Norman would receive 15 percent of the recovered artifacts with the remaining balance going to us.

Although Norman signed the contract, he tried again to change our minds. "You can try to dig the *Arabia*, but you won't reach her. No one else has. It's too deep, and there is too much groundwater. But if you want to shoot craps with your money, then come on ahead."

My brother drove Norman to the field where he believed the previous attemps had taken place. Using the magnetometer to pinpoint the *Arabia*'s exact location, Dave searched two hours before locating the boat.

After the farmer harvested the crops, my partners and I began outlining the boat. The drill rig spun the bit into the soft earth, and at a depth of 35 feet the drill struck the *Arabia* and shook violently. As with previous boats, we marked the location with a colored survey flag. Drilling only deep enough to touch the boat and not penetrate into the cargo area, we drilled for two days. Twenty-two flags later, we had completed the outline of the *Arabia*.

Core sampling came next. We were reluctant to damage valuable artifacts with blind drilling. However, we had to determine structural integrity of the boat and its depth, and we needed evidence of cargo.

The different layers of a steamboat say a lot about its condition. A core sample should contain a layer of pine from the main deck, then cargo stored below, and finally, white oak from the hull.

We hoped the *Arabia* had her upper decks intact and a cargo hold filled with merchandise. However, the first recovered core sample indicated quite the opposite. The steamer was void of any upper structure, and the sample showed no signs of pine decking or cargo, only oak from the hull. Our confidence shaken, we moved 70 feet back from the bow and drilled again. The second sample did little to boost our morale. The drill bit struck steel and penetrated no further.

By now, I was a veteran of disappointment. After three years working under difficult conditions, I had hoped the *Arabia* was the boat for us. My days of treasure hunting might be over if the next two core samples were inconclusive.

Our third attempt was 60 feet from the stern and 20 feet from the larboard or left side. The drill bit sliced into the boat and shook wildly, indicating an encounter with the main deck. As the bit penetrated deeper into the hull's cavity, the forceful vibration continued. After considerable effort and frustration, we removed the bit. The core sample indicated a large stack of two-inch thick pine lumber, apparently part of the *Arabia*'s cargo. Our hopes that the *Arabia* contained large quantities of good cargo were fading. With little enthusiasm, we repositioned the drill for a final sample. Drilling closer to the stern and starboard side, the drill bit struck the *Arabia* at 35 feet.

I sensed the tension between my partners; we were wavering between hope and disappointment. Jerry shifted his weight from one foot to the other. Dad had his hand in his pocket jingling his keys. Dave kept looking at his watch. As the core sampling bit began its rise to the surface, we were silent.

Laying the sample upon the ground, the inspection showed broken fragments of red glass, broken ironstone, and splintered wood.

"What is it?" I asked, dropping to my knees for a better look.

"We must have struck a box of new merchandise," Dad said.

Jerry grabbed his metal detector to search for signs of iron, and it beeped wildly as he passed it back and fourth across the mound of debris.

"The sample is full of metal fragments," Jerry said, while picking out two square nails. Groping through the mud with bare hands, we attempted to fashion together this shattered mystery. After several minutes of assembly we solved the puzzle. The broken glass was the remains of a delicate red goblet. The splintered wood revealed a branded crest displaying a lion, indicating a box that contained English Queensware. The crest of the lion, combined with the red goblet, gave us hope a cargo of fine dishes remained aboard the *Arabia*, a mere 35 feet beneath us.

The day ended with Jerry, Bob, Dave, and I leaning against our pickup trucks, parked directly over the steamboat *Arabia*. The time had come to choose a steamer and excavate or cut our losses and walk away. After three years of exploration and research, we discovered six of ten steamboats. The stakes were high in this modern-day treasure hunt.

As I stood above this ancient steamer, I knew that I was standing where others had stood, individuals with dreams and hopes, fears and uncertainties identical to ours. They, too, were men with determination, confident in their ability to reach and recover the cargo hidden aboard the *Arabia*. Looking from bow to stern, 171 feet in length, and starboard to larboard, 54 feet in width, I tried to imagine the treasure waiting for us below. We had come too far to retreat. We decided to excavate the Great White *Arabia*.

After sinking, the strong current of the Missouri River knocked off the upper decks of the Arabia.

Illustration by Dave Orf

Preparing to Dig

"If you want to shoot craps with your money, then come on ahead." The words of Norman Sortor stuck in my mind as my partners and I prepared to commit money, time, talent, and everything else necessary to capture the *Arabia*.

As a kid, I saw the Missouri River as a companion, exploring its banks, skipping rocks, and fishing its deep pools. Now I saw it as an opponent. The water, not sand and dirt, was the true obstacle between us and the *Arabia*'s treasure. This underground water, which forced a slurry of sand immediately into any void, had spoiled the previous salvage attempts. It was like trying to dig a ditch through a bed of quicksand.

Prior salvage attempts gave us valuable information on procedures that would not work. Our plan of attack demanded a new and innovative approach.

To overcome the immense flow of groundwater, my father designed a system using electric submersible pumps, commonly used for agricultural irrigation. Twelve pumps, each having a capacity of 1,000 gallons per minute, would circle the *Arabia* and remove the water from the ground faster than it poured in. The submersible pumps were 30 HP, 480 volts, with three diesel generators providing power.

Once my dad devised the de-watering strategy, we began assembling an arsenal of mechanical components: hundreds of feet of 14-inch diameter well casings and eight-inch diameter de-watering pipes, thousands of feet of wire, control boxes with motor starters and protectors, electric pumps, generators, and a 10,000-gallon fuel storage tank, to name but a few.

To install and assemble the de-watering system we needed a bulldozer, track loader, rubber tire loader, and a crane. The crane was so large that delivery by barge up the Missouri River was more cost effective than delivery by truck.

Looking for a landing site for the barge, Jerry and Dad slid a 16-foot jet boat into the river at Independence, Missouri, checked the fuel tank, and headed upriver. Though bucking a seven mile-per-hour current, the 20 mile journey to the excavation site took only one hour. If this trip had been a race against the *Arabia*, upriver and back, the jet boat's lead would stand at two hours.

On the river's south bank, they found a landing site with adequate depth for docking the barge. They noted the location and headed downriver towards home. Although the fuel gauge had dropped considerably during the trip upriver, the current now flowed in their favor. With ten miles remaining, the sun disappeared and the sky turned dark. Gliding past Kansas City, they savored the spectacular display of city lights reflected upon the water. Then the boat's engine coughed once and stopped. Jerry turned the key, but the engine spun with an unresponsive rhythm; they were out of gas.

"Nice night for a float trip," Jerry said with a smile.

"At least we're going in the right direction," Dad replied.

Drifting uncontrollably downstream, they debated whether to float to their destination or try to reach the bank and find additional fuel. Suddenly, a rumbling sound filled the air, and a bright spotlight illuminated the river. A massive line of barges rounded the bend. The tugboat operator pushing the huge load was unaware that Jerry and Dad were directly in his path!

The barges closed in with incredible speed. Dad and Jerry frantically dug through the boat and found a single oar and an old shovel. Paddling with all their strength, they tried to move the small boat out of the way, but the approaching vessel was moving too fast to elude. The tugboat's massive spotlights continued to sweep the river. Jerry and Dad yelled and waved their arms, but they remained unnoticed. The barges loomed overhead when, at the last moment, the spotlight struck them. The deafening air horns of the tug blasted into the night. With only a few feet of clearance the tug swung wide, narrowly missing the small vessel. Dad and Jerry held on as huge waves wildly rocked the boat.

"For a moment I thought there was going to be another sunken boat on the river," Dad said.

"That was too close. I think it's time to get some gas," Jerry replied. The barge disappeared upriver, leaving behind Jerry, Dad, and dwindling waves. As the river returned to its gentle nature, no evidence of the near tragedy remained except two hearts pounding loudly. Their narrow escape made finding gas a priority. One hard hour later, they reached the riverbank and walked two miles through thick brush and open fields to the gas station.

At the gas station, Jerry called his wife and asked for a ride back to the boat. Joan arrived in her brand new car and discovered the trip back to the river was more suited for a four-wheel drive. Forced to create her own road, Joan bumped and plowed through car-high weeds to the

Delivery of the 100-ton crane to the excavation was the first step in recovering the Arabia. *The crane was essential to assemble the de-watering system and lower the water wells into place.*

Photo by Dave Hawley

river. Joan dropped off Jerry, Dad, and a can of gas, and they soon had the boat fueled and underway. If Jerry and Dad were racing the *Arabia*, the old steamer would have crossed the finish line hours ahead, like the tortoise beating the hare.

Through October and into November 1988, our families gathered an arsenal of equipment to excavate the *Arabia*. Though the bitter cold months of winter were a difficult time to excavate the steamer, the water table was lower then and cold temperatures helped prevent deterioration of wet artifacts.

During our three years spent researching Missouri River steamboats, our families developed an all-encompassing passion for the river and the people it touched. Waiting below was a story frozen in time. The project was so significant we hired an archaeologist to document the *Arabia's* wooden structure, machinery, and cargo. Proper documentation was a critical step for future historical and scientific research.

We also arranged for security. News of the excavation would eventually leak out, and the curious might become a problem. The man for this job was Vince Dye. Vince and I had spent more time hunting and fishing together than we dared to admit. With a travel trailer for comfort, Vince, with the help of his faithful, but mangy bird dog, stood guard nightly.

While we prepared for the excavation, we talked about the *Arabia* as though she were already one of the family. "She" was probably looking up at us, feeling the earth shake with the constant arrival of trucks delivering supplies and needed equipment. She must be wondering about our chances.

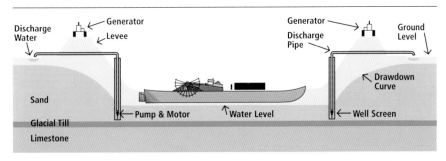

To salvage the Arabia *excavators needed the de-watering system to lower the ground water to a depth of 45 feet.*

Illustration by Dave Orf

CHAPTER 5

The Thrill of Discovery Begins

Installing Equipment

When I awoke on Sunday, November 13, 1988, the morning sun was two hours away. Today our families would break ground over the *Arabia*. Not since I was a kid on Christmas Eve had I felt such an overwhelming sense of excitement. With what felt like pure adrenaline flowing through my veins, I hastily dressed, kissed my sleeping wife good-bye, and stepped out into the pre-dawn. I arrived above the *Arabia* one hour later. Apparently, I was not the only one who could not sleep; my partners had arrived before I had.

With no previous experience drilling wells, and with little time to learn, we contacted the well drilling firm of Ro-Banks. The owners of the company, Roger and Charlotte Banks, agreed to drill the wells and were eager to assist in the excavation.

As Ro-Banks prepared to pierce the earth, others sat atop the bulldozer and track hoe, and fired the engines to life. No elected officials were present for speeches, no brass bands or ribbons to cut in celebration of this momentous event. There was just the eastern glow of the morning sun and the sound of heavy equipment moving downward towards the *Arabia*.

Throughout the day and well into the night, my partners and I labored. The work was physically exhausting. Assembling the de-watering system demanded brute strength. I could not remember the last time I worked so hard and felt so worn out, yet had so much fun. Together, we successfully drilled three 30-inch diameter wells to

left *Maneuvering the 65-foot de-watering well into position, the crane operator prepares to lower it into place.*

Photo by Beulah Sortor

right *Excavators assembled hundreds of feet of de-watering pipe to carry water from the dig site.*

Photo by Beulah Sortor

bedrock, assembled and lowered into place three 65-foot lengths of 14-inch well screen casing, and removed and stockpiled several hundred cubic yards of topsoil to be replaced at the end of the excavation.

All day the earth trembled as the equipment clattered by with a deafening sound, and the air was so heavy with diesel fuel I could taste it.

Despite dropping temperatures, seasonal rainfall, sleet, and occasional snow, the following days went well. By November 24, twelve days from the start, we had eight water wells drilled, well casings and pumps lowered into place, hundreds of feet of eight-inch pipe welded, motor protectors and control boxes wired, a 10,000-gallon fuel tank installed, generators and fuel lines connected, and a quarter-mile trench cut in the earth to carry water away from the site. All this, and we still had time left over for Thanksgiving dinner with our families.

The day after Thanksgiving, Dad hit the switch and fired up the generators and de-watering wells. Eight thousand gallons of water per minute roared to the surface, flowed through the trench, across the Sorter's farm, and spilled into the Missouri River. We stood on the edge of the excavation site and watched the water level above the *Arabia* drop. Yet by day's end, it had lowered only seven feet. The ground's stratum was obviously quite porous, allowing a much larger volume of water to flow into the excavation than we had expected. Although our planned de-watering system was still incomplete by four wells, we now questioned its ability to overcome the free-flowing groundwater beneath us.

We planned to uncover the stern of the *Arabia* first, since our core samples from that area were most promising. We hoped the stern of the *Arabia* held significant merchandise and would substantiate the viability of the excavation.

Moving towards the *Arabia*, I pondered the hardships of the steamboat traveler. I was in awe of the lives lost, hardships endured, and obstacles overcome by the passengers and crew. In an account from the *Louisville Journal*, dated May 21, 1849, the conditions are described:

> Boats have passed here, within whose narrow decks from three to five hundred human beings have been densely stowed or packed. The filth and stench on such boats are almost insupportable. The food used is of the most unwholesome kind, and the atmosphere which is breathed is impure in the extreme. Under such circumstances, nothing but disease and death can rightfully be expected....

In Louis C. Hunter's *Steamboats on the Western Rivers*, the account of a westward traveler is recorded: "Deck passengers were stowed like hogs on the lower deck of the steamer, where they were made to feel all the degradation of poverty in the brutal and disgraceful treatment they received from the petty officers belonging to the boat."

A letter from John James Ingalls, in 1858, describes the sounds on a riverboat created by the power of steam:

> There was a perfect pandemonium of sound. The dull thunder of the paddles; the rattling of the tiller chains, which ran directly over my head; the trembling of the boat, the panting roar of the escaping steam, which was so near I could almost detect the metamorphosis of water into force.

The fact that deck passengers endured these conditions demonstrated their desperation. Some journeyed only from the East Coast, while others came from the far corners of the world. Their courage and fortitude stands as a symbol to the power of hope.

By November 29, we had descended a mere 26 feet. Still, we were close, and I could sense the *Arabia*'s nearness.

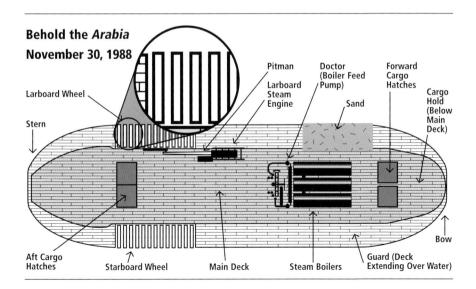

Behold the *Arabia*
November 30, 1988

Larboard Wheel
Stern
Pitman
Larboard Steam Engine
Doctor (Boiler Feed Pump)
Forward Cargo Hatches
Sand
Cargo Hold (Below Main Deck)
Aft Cargo Hatches
Starboard Wheel
Main Deck
Steam Boilers
Guard (Deck Extending Over Water)
Bow

On November 30, 1988, the trackhoe's bucket raked through the sand and struck a heavy, unidentified structure at a depth of 27 feet. Excitement swept the excavation site. Everyone gathered around, elbow to elbow, probing with long rods and digging through the sand. Within minutes the *Arabia*'s larboard paddle wheel, one board at a time, emerged. To hear our jubilant conversation, an outsider would think we had unearthed gold rather than wet oak that had been underground for 132 years.

Reaching down, I touched the *Arabia* for the first time, and a flood of emotions swept through me. Three years of research and walking countless miles of farm ground made that moment possible. I felt instantly justified. I was perched on the edge of history, and what a glorious sight it was.

Excavators uncover a board from the larboard paddle wheel. It was the first glimpse of the Great White Arabia. Photo by Greg Mackey

Our First Treasure
December 1, 1988

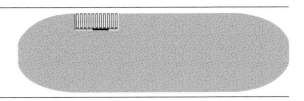

It was hard to concentrate on installing two more de-watering wells with the *Arabia* showing through the sand. By late afternoon, the wells were in and the four of us were eagerly shoveling sand from the larboard wheel.

With only a few inches of sand removed, we made a perplexing discovery: a white golf ball.

"I don't believe it. How did this get here?" Jerry asked, while scooping it from the sand.

Suddenly the sound of laughter filled the air, and, turning, we saw Jerry's two sons, Ron and Greg, amused beyond their control. Their actions made it obvious they were responsible. The day before both Ron and Greg were at the dig, and they apparently had hidden the ball as a joke.

"Keep your golf ball on the course," Jerry replied, while tossing it to Ron. "You about gave me a heart attack. I don't want to find anything down here newer than 1856."

Continuing to dig the old-fashioned way—with hand shovels—I frequently stepped back to capture the wheel's full image. The huge wheel tilted slightly at 30 degrees and had a diameter of 28 feet and a width of seven feet, six inches.

Unexpectedly, Jerry cried out, "Look, a shoe!" Nestled among the oak timbers of the mighty wheel was our first artifact! We threw down our shovels, and I scrambled to see this small yet momentous find.

With the greatest care, Dave lifted the shoe free. As he turned it over, the rest of us huddled around, scrutinizing this piece of history. The shoe showed notable signs of wear along the edges and sole, and we were amazed to see raised lettering on the bottom indicating a patent by the Goodyears Rubber Co., 1849.

At that moment, I knew why I was here. The gold and silver I often dreamed about suddenly meant nothing. I was reliving the wonder of childhood with the discovery of this rubber shoe now resting in my hands, and the unknown still hidden beneath my feet.

Over a century before, the violent current of the Missouri River broke off the upper spokes to the giant wheel.   **Photo By Beulah Sortor**

**Long Days and
Short Nights
December 2, 1988**

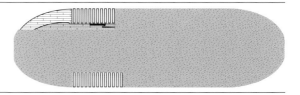

After more than two weeks fighting mud and sand, we had little to show for our sizable investment. The demanding schedule was wearing me down physically. Every morning I arose well before dawn. At the dig, we reassembled the water pumps taken apart the night before to prevent freezing and stretched out rolled up hoses. We used water hoses with adjustable pressure to gently wash away sand without damaging the artifacts. The water power necessary to move the sand and mud required us to lean forward to compensate for the back pressure. My hands cramped with pain as the hours passed. Winter winds whipping across the mouth of the excavation caused a blizzard of blowing sand in the pit. I wore goggles to protect my eyes. Sand finer than sugar invaded my ears, nose, and mouth. Despite the cold, my inner layers of clothing became soaked with sweat. If I took even a short break, the shivers set in. In spite of the hardships, we were not without success. For each de-watering pump installed, the water table dropped one foot closer to our treasure.

We removed more sand from on top of the *Arabia*, revealing the arching contour of the boat's structure and giving us new insights to its tragic demise. After sinking, the *Arabia* did not settle to a stop on the river's bed. Instead, the force of the river quickly eroded sand from beneath the steamer. Within one day, the *Arabia*'s hull countersunk completely into the river's muddy bottom. The bow and starboard side of the stern rested five feet lower than the middle section of the steamer. As time passed, river sand covered the *Arabia*'s hull, protecting it from the river above. However, the upper spokes of the paddle wheels and the upper decks of the majestic *Arabia* remained in the river's flow.

Now resting in silence, the larboard and starboard paddle wheels once pushed the Arabia *up the Missouri at a top speed of seven miles per hour.*   **Photo By Beulah Sortor**

The unmerciful force of the current, combined with the relentless bombardment of floating ice and logs, eventually knocked away the entire upper structure of the steamboat, scattering it downstream.

Our initial goal was to uncover the *Arabia's* stern, but the arching configuration of the hull brought the deck next to the larboard paddle wheel into view first. Using the water hoses to wash away sand, we stepped onto the *Arabia's* wet pine deck. We spoke as if perched upon hallowed ground. Not since the Missouri River swept over the deck 132 years before had anyone stood on this spot. The remnants of the past were scattered in all directions: pieces of cloth, broken shards of stoneware and glassware, pieces of a coffee grinder, and a cork for a bottle.

Twenty days into the excavation and with only the larboard side of the stern and both paddle wheels of the Arabia *uncovered, the enormity of the dig is apparent from the air.*
Photo by Greg Mackey

A Common Bond
December 3, 1988

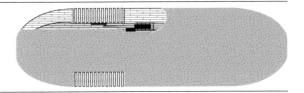

With clear skies, mild winds, and temperatures in the 60s, this Saturday was a perfect day for our families to visit.

Twelve children, eight-years-old and younger, burst onto the site. One moment the kids played at digging buried treasure, and then they gathered on large piles of sand and played King of the Mountain. They skidded, slid, and raced down 30-foot embankments that encircled the dig site. While keeping an eye on the children, Mom, Karen, my sister, Rita, and my brother's wife, Laurie, prepared a picnic lunch at the edge of the excavation. After drilling additional water wells and preparing the

Standing on the main deck of the Arabia, *Greg Hawley shares a discovery with Norman Sortor and his daughter, Patricia Gates. For the first time since Norman's grandfather, Elisha Sortor, bought the land in 1864, a Sortor finally touched the* Arabia. *From left, they are: Norman Sortor, Patricia Gates (Norman's daughter), Greg Hawley.*   **Photo by Kenneth Gates**

Two families brought together by a common dream of finding buried treasure. On the back row is Greg Hawley. Front row, from left are: Bob Hawley, Patricia Gates, Norman Sortor, Beulah Sortor, Dave Hawley.   **Photo by Kenneth Gates**

pumps for insertion into the water table, we stopped for lunch and spent a rare moment with our families.

Norman Sortor, with his wife, Beulah, daughter, Patricia Gates, and son-in-law, Kenneth Gates, dropped by. Just before the dig began, Norman was diagnosed with cancer. He had previously been too weak to visit the excavation site, but on this day Norman jauntily stepped from the car. He strolled to the edge of the excavation with his daughter and wife on each arm, and stared down into the depths of his land, seeing at long last the Great White *Arabia*.

Norman wanted to get closer. He was too weak to walk down the steep roadway into the excavation, so we provided an alternate mode of transportation—the bulldozer. Norman, Beulah, and Patricia climbed into the bucket and bumped and rattled their way down into the site.

Within minutes, Norman was standing upon the main deck of the *Arabia*.

"Have you found any whiskey?" Norman asked me with a smile.

"I wish we had," I said.

"Well if you find it," said Norman, "bring me some. I've always wanted to taste that whiskey."

I felt honored to stand with Norman. For three generations, the Sortor family had plowed, planted, and harvested their crops from this land. On many occasions, Norman had worked the farm with his father, Fred Sortor. During those days afield, Norman listened intently as Fred told of the *Arabia* and the treasure just out of their reach.

The *Arabia* brought our families together, intertwining their legacy with our quest for buried treasure.

Steam Power
December 4, 1988

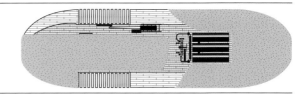

Twenty-three days after breaking ground, the spring in my legs had gone. I dragged myself out of bed and splashed cold water on my face. Peeking with one eye into the mirror, I wondered who that frazzled and unshaven man was staring back at me. The elements of winter and the constant influx of water into the excavation site were taking their toll.

Each day provided a visual feast that surpassed the previous day. With both paddle wheels partially exposed, it was clear the river had not been kind to the *Arabia* after the sinking. Having at one time proudly floated upon the muddy waters of the Missouri, she now appeared crushed and defeated. Her timbers were twisted and beaten, waterlogged, and violently broken, betrayed by the waters that once buoyed her.

Despite the ravages of the river, evidence of fine craftsmanship was apparent. Massive timbers were joined so precisely that modern technology would find duplicating the joints a challenge.

Four days of washing uncovered two 60-foot wooden structures that braced, not only the towering paddle wheels, but also provided a foundation for the *Arabia*'s enormous steam engines. When we uncovered the steam engine supports, only the larboard engine remained. Salvagers, probably fueled by an insurance incentive, had removed the starboard engine within days of the *Arabia* sinking.

Each paddle wheel had a single piston engine with a power stroke of six feet. A connecting rod, called a pitman arm, connected the piston to the side-wheel crank. Steam intake and exhaust valves delivered steam to the piston in one moment, shut it down in the next, then vented it upward to the atmosphere at the completion of the stroke. Long iron rods triggered valve timing by moving back and forth against eccentric cams located on the paddle wheel's iron shaft. The larboard heat exchanger, which sat above the engine and toward the paddle wheel, preheated boiler water by utilizing hot exhaust steam vented from the engine. With a double wall, cold river water flowed around the outer jacket of the inner drum, while steam passed through the interior core before venting to the outside. Copper pipes delivered the slightly tempered water into the steam boilers.

We were washing sand from the forward portion of the engine when we discovered a horse shoe hanging from a single nail on the engine's wooden support. Horse shoes are traditionally a sign of good luck, but

The larboard (left) engine displays the face of what appears to be the Roman god, Bacchus, lord of the vineyard. With no visible manufacturer's mark, the origin of this engine is still a mystery. It is an interesting coincidence that the Vulcan Iron and Machine Works, an engine-building company using Vulcan, the Roman god of fire and iron as a symbol, operated next to the Pringle Boat-Building Company.   **Photo by Greg Hawley**

only when the ends are pointing up—holding in their good luck. Unfortunately for the *Arabia*, this horse shoe was pointing down. We also uncovered a haunting image of Bacchus, the god of wine. Cast in iron on the end of the engine's cylinder, the god's face featured leaves and grapes for hair, and the eyes had a distant look.

During our days of washing, we uncovered the "doctor" and boilers resting halfway up the *Arabia*'s main deck. The "doctor" is a small steam engine that supplied the driving force to pumps that fed water into the boilers. Its reputation for remedying the ills of cantankerous engines and boilers is how the "doctor" earned its name. Consisting of a vertical engine tied directly to a cross beam crank and massive fly wheel, it commanded two lift pumps that forced water into the heat exchanger, and two feed pumps that drove water into the boilers against steam pressure reaching 90 pounds per square inch.

Three horizontal boilers rose eight feet above the *Arabia*'s main deck. Running parallel with the steamer, each boiler measured 24 feet in length and three feet in diameter. Cast iron doors for fueling or

A steam driven water pump, known as the "doctor," provided river water to the boilers.
Photo by Dave Hawley

The Arabia's *boilers consisted of three large boiler tanks measuring 24 feet in length and three feet in diameter. Firemen, responsible for fueling boilers, stoked the fire box with up to 30 cords of wood for every 24 hours of operation.* **Photo by Dave Hawley**

removing burnt wood or ash from the fire box hung on the forward end. This configuration was traditional construction for steamboats. The forward motion of the steamer helped to induce air into the fire box for better combustion.

One fire door remained open. Apparently workers were adding fuel when the steamboat struck the snag. The fire box had a brick lining and held a stack of partially burnt wood. The heat, smoke, and hot gases emitted from this fire traveled beneath the boilers before turning back through duel interior flues, then shot upward through massive stacks— long since washed away—that stretched 60 feet skyward.

A two-man pump with a rubber hose attached sat next to the boilers on the starboard side. Crewmen used this pump for washing down the decks, priming the boilers for the start of each day, and putting out fires caused by shooting sparks and runaway embers.

Now, when I walked into the pit, I felt the presence of the *Arabia* not only beneath me, but above and all around me. The steamer's twin paddle wheels towered overhead, while the larboard engine, steam doctor, and boilers lined the boundaries of our work.

Workers aboard the Arabia *used this hand pump to prime boilers, wash down the deck, and put out fires caused by shooting sparks.* **Photo by Dave Hawley**

Uncovering
the Stern

The Magic Barrel
December 5, 1988

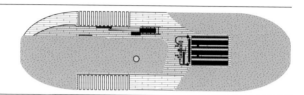

leven pumps were now removing groundwater from below while
we washed away sand from above. At 3:15 P.M., on December 5,
the top of an oak barrel, two feet in diameter, came into view.
The barrel rested on the main deck of the *Arabia* between the
paddle wheels.

"I can't wait to see inside that barrel," Dad said. He put down the
hose and we crowded around. Jerry pried open the lid, and inside was a
glistening assortment of fine dishes and glassware. Everyone hollered
with excitement. Peripheral work ceased at the excavation as our shouts
drew the attention of everyone.

Kneeling in the sand, Dad lifted free a large ironstone bowl. The rest
of us nearly got in a fight trying to hold it. Jerry was the first to grasp
the bowl. Holding it tightly to his chest, he ran to his nearby truck,
climbed in, and locked the door. I could not believe it. He cradled the
bowl like it was his first born. Occasionally he looked up and smiled
from the sanctuary of his vehicle. Only more dishes coaxed him out.

We surrounded the barrel and took turns forcing our hands blindly
into the mud. Most of the dishes were below the water table and only
by touch could we find them. Taking turns lying on our stomachs, we
extended our arms into the barrel. With constant upward pressure the
mud loosened its grip on the items, and we lifted them free. Although
caked with mud, they were still beautiful. The variety of dishes and
glassware amazed us: imported Davenport Ironstone with blue
decorative patterns of Cypress and Friburg, plates and bowls

manufactured by Wedgwood, delicate glass whale oil lamps, syrup pitchers and salt dips, clear tumblers, spice jars and ink wells, and a decorative flowered teapot with 19 matching cups.

Dad got on the car phone and called my mom. "You've got to come down and see what we've found," Dad said.

"I can't," Mom replied. "I've got chili on the stove."

"Well turn that stove off, and get down here," Dad said in a firm tone. At that moment, Mom knew we had found something extraordinary.

left *Davenport Ironstone, Friburg pattern*

Photo by Greg Hawley

right *Tea set origin unknown*

Photo by Greg Hawley

More calls were made, and soon our wives arrived. They were so excited when they saw how beautiful the items were. Without a sink and running water, they knelt on the ground and started washing the dishes in a pool of groundwater. They laughed and talked as they cleaned. Never before had I seen anyone have such a good time washing dishes.

The evening had overtaken us, and the sky was black. Seven hours had elapsed since discovering this magic barrel.

We went to Jerry's house and continued to clean well into the next morning. Scattered upon his kitchen table, chairs, and counters were

left *An excavator holds a piece of J. Wedgwood Ironstone China.*

right *J. Wedgwood Hallmark*

Photos by Greg Hawley

right *Bob Hawley proudly holds two delicate pieces of Friburg Ironstone China imported from England. Excavators recovered 178 pieces of China and glassware from a single oak barrel.*

Photo by Greg Hawley

178 of the most beautiful pieces of finery we had ever seen.

It is very interesting to note that Josiah Wedgwood founded the family pottery in Staffordshire, England, in 1759. Since the company's inception, Wedgwood potters set the standard for quality in the production of earthenware. *Wedgwood A Collectors Guide*, by Peter Williams, records the success of Wedgwood that inspired several potters to employ markings meant to mislead the unknowing buyer. As a result, some Wedgwood discovered aboard the *Arabia* displays the misleading name J. WEDGWOOD.

John Wood of Burslem, England, unethically used the middle name Wedge, which legally allowed him to print or press the word WEDGWOOD, with a slight gap between the two words. John Wedge Wood was the son of John Wood II (1778-1848), of the pottery family of Burslem. John Wedge Wood (1813-1857) operated their business at the Hadderidge Potbank in Burslem. The original Wedgwood firm used only the word WEDGWOOD, without the initial J., and without the slight gap.

Over Budget
December 6-7, 1988

Prior to the excavation, we had estimated that $250,000 was necessary to complete the dig. Unfortunately, we had spent nearly the entire amount just reaching the *Arabia*. As we installed the twelfth well on December 6 and 7, we realized we needed financial help. Having shared stories of our adventure with friends and relatives, they purchased 15 shares of our company for $150,000. The funds helped pay for an additional $20,000 generator, pumps, well casings, and a growing fuel bill.

With the twelfth well on line, the water table dropped an additional foot. Unfortunately, water was still eight feet above the stern section. We ordered additional de-watering equipment and eagerly awaited its arrival.

My work at the excavation seemed nonstop. I gave up family dinners, Sunday church, and sacrificed the pleasure of reading bedtime stories to my kids. Arriving home late at night, I looked in at my sleeping children. I knew that no treasure could ever buy back the time I had lost with my family.

Caring For the Treasure
December 8, 1988

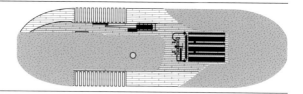

Despite wind chills below zero, I felt warmed by new discoveries protruding through the sand: wooden kegs, grinding wheels, an assortment of partially exposed wooden crates, wagon wheels, and axles. Walking on the thin layer of sand covering the *Arabia*, I watched where I stepped. A misplaced foot could destroy a priceless artifact and its story.

With the *Arabia*'s oaken timbers partially exposed and a sampling of cargo recovered, we gradually realized the complicated nature of our endeavor. Underwater and beneath the earth, the *Arabia* and its cargo had rested for 132 years in an anaerobic (oxygen-free) environment. This lack of oxygen, combined with constant temperatures, no light, and a neutral soil pH of seven, helped preserve the artifacts.

In spite of the favorable environment, the *Arabia* and its contents had been damaged. Previous research had indicated that water dissolves strength-giving cellulose from wood, leaving it waterlogged and weak. If allowed to air-dry without appropriate preservation, wood from the *Arabia* would shrink and crack from lack of support.

Ironically, my family and I had trained all our lives for this moment. The first step in caring for the *Arabia* collection was stabilizing the artifacts. We did this by controlling humidity and temperature, something we did every day in our refrigeration business.

Jerry Mackey was also an intricate part of stabilizing the artifacts. He operated several restaurants and provided large walk-in coolers and freezers for storage. We also converted his food commissary into a lab to process our discoveries.

We satisfied our need for underwater storage for wood by leasing 5,000 square feet of underground area in a limestone cave. Underground storage enabled us to use large quantities of water without fear of damaging the rented space.

We continually hosed down the wooden artifacts until we could transport them back to the processing lab in Independence, Missouri.

After inspection, we placed these fragile items in underwater storage or in freezers.

Leather artifacts also suffered similar damage. The oils used for tanning had long since dissolved. If allowed to air-dry, the leather shrank and became irreversibly stiff. We cleaned off the mud and froze the leather in blocks of ice.

Textiles that survived beneath the water were made of protein; beaver hair, wool, and silk. For long-term stabilization, freezing seemed appropriate. However, we decided not to freeze the fabrics in blocks, fearing the strenuous process of expansion during the initial freeze would damage the material. We drained textiles of excess water, then quickly froze them at -10 degrees Fahrenheit. The final procedure involved encapsulating the fabrics in ice by misting water onto the already frozen surface.

The assortment of artifacts frozen in Jerry's freezer surprised health department officials inspecting his restaurant. They agreed to ignore them, as long as Jerry did not place them on a bun and serve them to his customers.

Artifacts made of iron alloys, such as wrought iron, cast iron, and steel, had little active corrosion. However, if left wet and unattended, metal suddenly exposed to the adverse environment of sunlight, fluctuating temperatures, and oxygen began to rust rapidly.

After initial recovery, we cleaned metal items of all loose material and dried them with soft towels. For long-term storage, we placed these artifacts in the basements of our homes where we controlled humidity and temperature.

Artifacts made of rubber, though durable in appearance, deteriorate through oxidation. To minimize deterioration, we froze rubber items in blocks of ice.

Unearthing the *Arabia* was fulfilling our wildest dreams. Yet, with the recovery of these fragile treasures, our families faced the difficult task of caring for and nuturing our discoveries.

Bones of a Victim
December 9, 1988

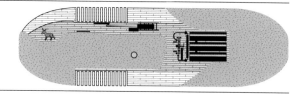

We were still seven days away from the delivery of additional de-watering pumps, generators, and support equipment.

Despite our battle against the water, the *Arabia* continued to surprise us. Hosing down the stern, we exposed a saddle horn. Carefully, my partners and I washed away sand to reveal the saddle. As its shape emerged, a bizarre surprise greeted us; a skeleton protruded from beneath the saddle. At first we thought it was a horse, but closer inspection of the bones indicated it was a mule.

Throughout the morning and into the afternoon we toiled to unveil the entire skeleton and solve this mystery. Lying on its right side, the mule had rested undisturbed for 132 years, saddled and bridled with the bit firmly clinched in his teeth. Unfortunately, the owner of the mule had left the bridle reins tied to a heavy piece of sawmill equipment. The iron equipment was like an anchor around the poor animal's neck. When the *Arabia* disappeared into the muddy Missouri, the mule had no choice but to follow. The identity of the mule's owner remains a mystery, despite the clues left behind.

The owner's bedroll rested behind the saddle with a small block plane rolled up inside. A tin cup and slightly bent tin plate rested on the mule's hip, and was possibly held in place by a cotton knapsack long since dissolved. The initials A. P. were scratched on the bottom of the cup. We stood over the mule, awestruck by this incredible discovery, and wondered why the animal's owner did not loosen the simple knot?

Later, we discovered an article printed in a St. Joseph newspaper, just after the *Arabia* sank, in which the owner of the mule attested he tried his best to get the mule off the *Arabia*, but it was too stubborn. This story seems unlikely, since we found the reins tied to the sawmill equipment. The owner, apparently ashamed at having left his mule tethered to the boat, made up this story. He could not have known we would catch him in a lie 132 years later.

A descendent of one passenger on the *Arabia* has also provided insights into the mule's death. Joan Thayer's great, great grandmother, Gertrude Kohlman, then age 23, had watched the mule drown. According to the story passed down through her family, Gertrude was eating dinner when the *Arabia* hit the snag. As the steamer sank, she assisted a small child to safety on the upper decks. Gertrude noticed the mule standing on the stern with water rising around him. The mule showed no signs of fear as the water's buoyancy lifted him off the deck. The mule still did not panic until the reins tied to the equipment began to pull his nose into the water. Only then did the mule bleat wildly and

left *The only fatality aboard the* Arabia *was a mule. Found on the stern, the owner left the reins tied to heavy sawmill equipment. The mule had little choice but to go down with the* Arabia.

Photo by Greg Hawley

right *Gertrude Kohlman, at the age of 23, was eating dinner aboard the* Arabia *when it struck the snag. Taken ashore at Parkville, Missouri, the small town became her permanent home.*

Photo courtesy of the family

thrash about in the water, trying to break free. Within moments the mule disappeared. Gertrude was quite distressed having heard the mule's cries and witnessing its death. She stayed in Parkville after the *Arabia* sank, and later married Joaquin Busch. Gertrude worked as a housekeeper in Parkville, and had three children. The mule's death made such an impression on Gertrude that she told the story often to her children and grandchildren. She died in January 1901.

From the first day I saw the mule with its reins tied to the sawmill equipment, I have wondered why the mule did not break free. An animal of its size could have snapped the reins with one powerful jerk. This question is now solved with Gertrude's story. Apparently, the mule did not panic until after the water lifted it off the deck. By then it was too late. His hooves no longer touched the deck; and with nothing to push against, he could not break the thin leather reins.

The mule found on the *Arabia* was not the only death associated with the steamer. During its travels on America's rivers, a total of four people had lost their lives while on the boat.

According to a case argued before the Missouri Supreme Court and the related depositions, the first fatality was a 13-year-old slave.

On October 5, 1853, James H. Johnston and a cargo of 12 slaves boarded the steamer *Arabia* for a trip on the Mississippi, from Paducah, Kentucky, to St. Louis, Missouri. Master John Woodburn was in command of the steamer.

On October 6, at 10:00 A.M., the *Arabia* needed fuel for the boilers and brought alongside two flatboats loaded with wood. Tying off the flatboats, one on each side of the bow, the *Arabia* continued upriver.

Michael Kirkpatrick, acting as second mate, ordered Johnston's 12 slaves to come forward and help load the wood.

The youngest of the slaves was Napoleon, alias "Pole." He wore striped pants and a hat, and besides being looked upon as a smart kid, was spry and stout in his actions. Kirkpatrick split the slaves into two groups, one group for each flatboat, with Pole working on the starboard side. It was important to unload the wood in a systematic fashion so as not to tilt the steamer. The pace of the work was brisk. Young Pole soon found it difficult to keep up with the older men, and Kirkpatrick ordered Pole to step aside. Pole watched the men stack the wood higher and higher. Suddenly, the wood pile began to tumble. To avoid the falling lumber, Pole stepped backwards, tripped, and fell into the Mississippi. The cry, "Man overboard!" filled the air as the alarm bell rang and the steamer *Arabia* came to a halt. The first mate, Thomas W. Rea, II, ran for the steamer's yawl (hardly a life boat); and with the help of two deck hands, he lowered it into the Mississippi and rowed downstream searching in vain for young Napoleon.

Johnston decided to sue those responsible for the death of his slave. He paid two dollars per day for deckhands and passengers to stay in St. Louis and give legal depositions.

On January 8, 1855, the lawsuit came to trial. Master of the *Arabia*, John Woodburn, stated during his testimony: "The plaintiff (Johnston) brought the Negroes aboard without asking any permission of me. I knew nothing of their being aboard until the next day after they came aboard. Even when this boy was lost, I did not know that he belonged to the plaintiff. I don't think I ever spoke to the plaintiff until after the boy fell over board. If the plaintiff had told me that he had the Negroes aboard, and that he held the boat responsible for them, I would not have them aboard."

Despite the testimony of Master John Woodburn, the jury ultimately awarded James H. Johnston the sum of $904 for the loss of young Napoleon.

Three other deaths occurred from cholera. On June 6, 1855, the steamboat *Arabia*, loaded with civilian passengers, military supplies, and 109 officers and men of the Second Infantry, departed St. Louis.

In 1855, an outbreak of Asiatic cholera had spread quickly throughout the country. Infected travelers transferred the disease along thoroughfares leading first to major cities and finally to remote regions of the country. The *Richfield Enterprise*, dated May 25, 1855, reported that one day into the journey cholera broke out aboard the *Arabia* and took the life of a civilian known as Mr. Dave, of Independence, Missouri. According to the Muster Roll of the Second Regiment of the U.S. Infantry dated August 10, 1855, the other victims were a military musician, Arnold Stamm, and Private John Rice. The troops may have brought the deadly disease with them from Pennsylvania.

Fighting the Water
December 10 - 12, 1988

The greater part of the next three days was spent installing necessary equipment. We delivered a trailer to the excavation site and converted it into a make-shift lab for the preliminary cleaning of artifacts. Giving the artifacts a light cleaning before transporting them to the lab in Independence saved us time at day's end. We also installed a submersible water pump to remove wash water. The amount of water used to wash sand off the *Arabia* had become a major problem. As if we did not have enough water to worry about, our wash water would not soak back into the sand quickly enough. By midday, water had climbed up to our knees and hindered our progress. We used the pump to pull wash water from the excavation pit and deliver it up and out of the area. However, even this was fraught with problems. The pump had more than enough power to push our wash water through a four-inch hose up and over the steep walls of the excavation pit, but heavy river sand settled in the hose. Every hour we had to shut off the pump and clean out the sand. At times, the hose was so tightly packed with sand it took nearly an hour

Excavators uncovered the stern of the Arabia *less than one month into the excavation, but the water table remained too high to enter the cargo hold.* Photo by Dave Hawley

to clean.

Howling winds and temperatures in the teens made working outside miserable. Our fingers, ears, noses, and toes burned from the cold. Only the sight of boxes peeking through the sand made the frigid temperatures tolerable.

A Meal Never Eaten
December 13, 1988

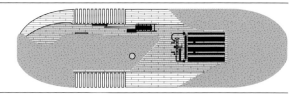

Morning temperatures were an unusual 32 degrees with a projected high of 60 degrees; perfect digging weather.

With water hoses and shovels, my partners and I aggressively moved sand. Our search for new discoveries was not a long one. Dave uncovered a large wooden box, three feet by four feet, resting near the starboard paddle wheel. As I dug away additional sand, I saw a small hinged door secured with a padlock.

"There must be something valuable inside," I said. Kneeling beside the husky box, Dad loosened the door with a pry bar and gently swung

right *A knee from an ox, bones of a pig, and one open can of peaches represent the Arabia's "last supper."*

Photo by Greg Hawley

left *The* Arabia's *ice box.*

Photo by Dave Hawley

it open. We crowded around. At first, all I could see was sand, but with a gentle spray of water the treasure inside came into view: a peach can, copper tray, and bones. We had discovered the *Arabia*'s ice box. The peach can, with its lid pried open, still contained peach pits. The copper platter, for cutting and preparing meat, had a recessed area at one end for the collection of blood and showed knife marks deeply cut into the

Doorknobs, locks, and keys discovered aboard the Arabia *numbered in the thousands. They reflected the need for building supplies on the frontier. The white doorknobs are made of porcelain, while the brown doorknobs are made of clay.* Photo by Greg Hawley

bottom. The bones inside were from an ox and pig. We had discovered the *Arabia*'s "last supper," a meal never eaten.

Next we uncovered a large oak barrel. With each barrel, I felt a rush of excitement. I watched as Dad pried off the lid. The barrel was filled to the brim with doorknobs, locks, keys, hinges, and screws. We carried load after load of door hardware to our trucks, an estimated 2,000-pounds of white porcelain doorknobs and brown knobs with swirling patterns of clay resembling marble, padlocks, square door locks, bit keys up to four and a half inches in length, door hinges, and the screws to mount them all.

A Barrel of Fun
December 14, 1988

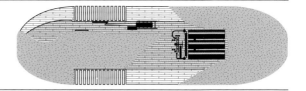

Despite the bitter weather, Jerry, Mom, Dad, my brother, several investors, and I were all at the excavation site. No one seemed to notice the cold. The *Arabia* provided spellbinding entertainment.

Using the wash hoses to remove sand, it was not long before another barrel came into view. Everyone gathered around, eager to see inside.

"I bet it's more hardware," Jerry said.

"Probably whiskey," Dad replied.

Half the fun before opening any box or barrel was speculating on the contents. The other half was lifting the lid quickly, peeking inside, and closing it again before my partners could see. This drove them crazy.

Loosening the barrel's top, I bent down slightly, lifted the lid, glanced inside, and closed it. With a knowing look, I leaned defiantly on the barrel and stared at my less than amused friends and family. They moved towards me, and I sensed the barrel's lid was not the only thing they intended to lift out of the way.

"It's full of dishes," I said with an upbeat tone, taking a precautionary step backwards. As if moving in for the kill, they circled the barrel and lifted the lid. The barrel was filled with Ironstone dishware. The original straw packing draped across the dishes like spaghetti. There was a moment of silence, then Jerry carefully nudged an exposed dish. They

Jerry and Joan Mackey wash away mud from pieces of Ironstone dishware. Excavators recovered 239 pieces from one oak barrel.   **Photo by Greg Hawley**

were so tightly packed he could not budge them. Dad had to spray water and clean away the mud before Jerry could lift out the first dish. For hours we carried away pure white round dishes and blue shell-edged earthenware, serving dishes, bowls with acorns adorning the lids, and rectangular platters. We recovered 239 pieces of Ironstone dishware from this one barrel.

Before leaving the excavation with our new treasures, we gave them a light washing, wrapped each piece in paper, and nestled them into five-gallon plastic buckets and cardboard boxes.

Driving back to Independence, we were sensitive to every bump in the road. We called ahead to our support team—our wives. When we entered the lab, we were surrounded by 50 plastic buckets containing 2,000-pounds of doorknobs, locks, keys and hinges; previous discoveries were piling up.

For a moment, I felt overwhelmed. Then I rolled up my shirt sleeves and began to clean. It was fun to see the dishware sparkle like new again. After all, they were new.

The work day continues into the night, as Florence Hawley, investor Joyce Porterfield, and Joan Mackey clean artifacts from the Arabia. **Photo by Dave Hawley**

We shut down the lab just after midnight. Tomorrow's work day would begin in less than six hours.

A Child's Loss
December 15, 1988

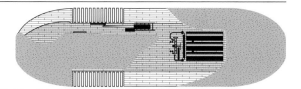

Having excavated down to the water table, we had reached our productive limits. It was time to drill more wells.

The well drilling firm of Ro-Banks arrived just before dawn. The drilling and setting of wells required everyone's combined efforts. We spent the next three days sinking wells while enduring sinking temperatures. Still, we took an occasional break to look for more treasure.

On one of those breaks we discovered a box between the paddle wheels on the main deck. The box had belonged to a passenger and contained a large assortment of J. Heath Ironstone dishware and other westbound essentials: tin bowls, cups, a flour scoop, spice grate with nutmeg still inside, a rolling pin, a spice rack with bottles containing spices, and two sea shells. Sitting in the seat of a toy tin rickshaw were seven marbles, two made of china, the others of clay.

I imagined the despair and hopelessness this mother and child felt after losing their precious belongings to the river. The mother was suddenly without her kitchen essentials, while the child lost seven marbles, two sea shells, and a tin toy.

Looking at this child's modest possessions, I found myself a little ashamed. My children had so much in comparison. To open their closet door at home was to risk a possible avalanche of toys.

Although the toys we found in this box were not essential to the family, my heart strings were tugged most for the child's loss.

Mark Twain observed in *Which Was the Dream*: "Nothing that grieves us can be called little: by the laws of proportion a child's loss of a doll and a king's loss of a crown are events of the same size."

Though meager possessions by modern standards, these toys were a severe loss for a frontier-bound child.
    Photo by Greg Hawley

Dangerous Work
December 16, 1988

Installing de-watering wells was slow and dangerous work. After Ro-Banks drilled the first hole to bedrock, we moved the crane forward to set the long steel well casing. Sixty-five feet of eight-inch steel pipe dangled vertically from the crane's cable, swinging back and forth like a pendulum. As on previous wells, my partners and I stood around the hole preparing to guide the pipe into place. But this time the crane's cable suddenly began to unreel.

"Watch out!" my father yelled. The dangling pipe fell with the cable and slammed into the ground, narrowly missing both us and the hole, before unhooking from the boom cable.

The pipe stood erect, momentarily balancing itself. We stood like statues, too scared to run, not knowing which direction the pipe would topple. Then, as if in slow motion, it tilted and began to fall. We scrambled to the south, our heavy boots covered with partially frozen, slippery mud, preventing a quick and easy escape. Up and over pipe, cable, and equipment we scrambled as if a bear were on our tail. Behind us we heard a thundering crash as the pipe smashed into the ground where we had stood. I gave the crane operator a stern glance, but he just smiled and shrugged his shoulders from the safety of the crane's reinforced cab. When I suggested we trade places on the next well, his smile disappeared.

We worked intently on the installation of de-watering wells despite bone-freezing wind chills of 17 degrees below zero. Later in the day, we started clearing away sand over the *Arabia*'s bow. Suddenly, the bulldozer uncovered timbers 30 feet above the *Arabia* on the forward end. It was an odd place to hit anything. Using hand shovels, we found a square wooden structure, remnants of an early salvage attempt. The framework had an inside measurement of five feet, barely enough room for anyone to work. Digging downward and around the outside of the structure, we found it descended only four feet. This bit of construction, which had never reached the *Arabia*, could have belonged to the Henry Tobener and Robert Treadwell salvage of 1877, the first recorded salvage.

Henry Tobener and his partner Robert Treadwell reached the *Arabia*,

Front row, from left are: Frank, Elizabeth (mother), Elizabeth (youngest daughter), Henry (father), and Edward. Back row: Rose, William, Frances, Robert, Emma, and Laura.
Courtesy of Fay and Lester Oberholtz

but only succeeded in recovering one case of wet hats. Henry spent $2,000 trying unsuccessfully to recover the legendary whiskey aboard the *Arabia*, and was bitter about the expenditure until the day he died.

The above picture features the Tobener family. Today the photo hangs proudly in the *Arabia* museum and is the catalyst for many stories.

Sitting between Henry and his wife, Elizabeth, is their youngest daughter, ten-year-old Elizabeth. In 1887, time exposure for indoor photography was extremely slow. The subjects had to sit like statues to prevent a blurred image. Henry, aware of his daughter's fidgety tendencies, insisted she fold her arms across her chest and tuck her hands out of sight. He instructed young Elizabeth to pull her legs back and wrap them around the legs of the bench. Then, Henry used his right leg to wedge Elizabeth tightly against her mother. Henry kept Elizabeth still, but lost any hope of a smile.

From the moment our families began looking for sunken steamers, our efforts seemed predestined. At times, I believe we succeeded in spite of ourselves. The picture of the Tobener family represents just one of the many events that seemed to be more than mere coincidence.

One hot day in August, two years after the excavation ended, my mother called me through the truck's two-way radio and asked me to make another service call before the day concluded. Two hours later, I was ringing the door bell at the residence of Fay and Lester Oberholtz. Fay met me at the door and showed me around the house while telling me about the air conditioner. I solved the problem and climbed into my truck, but Fay came to the door and waved me back inside.

"My husband, Lester, became very sick yesterday. We don't know what's wrong, but he's insisting that he speak with you." Stepping through the bedroom door, I saw Mr. Lester Oberholtz. A man in his eighties, Lester was laying in bed, flat on his back, and white as a sheet.

"I just had to talk to you, young man," Lester said in a weak tone. "I've been reading about you and the other families digging the *Arabia*, and I just wanted to tell you that it was my grandfather who tried to dig the *Arabia* first."

"The Tobener family?" I asked intrigued.

"That's correct," Lester replied.

I pulled up a chair and for the next hour we talked about his family, their excavation, our excavation, and the *Arabia*. I tore up the bill for the service call.

"Hanging on the wall behind you is a picture you'll find interesting," Lester said, pointing with a shaky finger. I stepped up close, my nose nearly touching the glass, and stared into the eyes of Henry Tobener.

"The older couple in the front row are my grandparents, and the little girl sitting between them is Elizabeth, my mother," Lester explained. "She was only ten years old when that picture was taken, and she died in 1966, in this very room."

Before I could comment, Lester asked, "Would you like to have that picture for your museum?"

"I would be honored to have it," I said.

"You probably have your truck with you," Lester said. "Why don't you take it now."

"No," I decided. "This picture is just a picture unless there is a story to go with it. Lester, could you write down any information you might feel is important regarding this photo and the Tobener family? When you finish, call me, and I'll come get the picture and, most importantly, the story."

Lester and I continued to talk when the phone rang. Fay picked up the phone on the night stand, but abruptly set the receiver on the dresser and went in the other room to talk in private.

Fay then came back into the bedroom, hung up the phone, and said to Lester, "He sure was embarrassed."

"Who was that, dear?" Lester asked.

"That was a man with the museum in Kansas City. Don't you remember, Lester? We offered them this picture nearly five years ago, and they never did come and get it."

Turning his head toward me, Lester said. "Greg, suddenly you have some competition. Maybe you'd like to take the picture with you after all?"

"No," I insisted, "you call me when you're done with the story."

Two weeks later I received a phone call from Lester Oberholtz. He had completed the writing. Then, two days later I received another call from Fay—Lester had passed away.

Personal Belongings
December 17 - 18, 1988

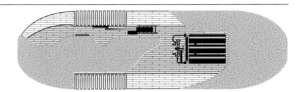

For the next two days, we worked primarily on the de-watering system. We lowered four additional wells into place, assembled the de-watering pumps, installed motor controls, and welded together the hundreds of feet of eight-inch pipe necessary to take water away from the dig site.

Although we continued to work on the de-watering system, we felt an urgency to uncover areas of the *Arabia* that were above the water table. After all, it was almost impossible not to explore for a few hours each day.

Warm weather brought out all our friends, relatives, and even a few folks that nobody knew. I didn't mind the extra visitors. Anyone who was willing to work was welcome.

After lunch, we stretched out the wash hoses and began removing

Operating around the clock, the de-watering system pumped huge amounts of discharge water from the ground before flowing across the Sortor's farm and back to the river.
Photo by Beulah Sortor

sand from the larboard side. My brother-in-law, Mark Scherer, volunteered to help wash sand. Leaning into the hose to help compensate for the powerful back pressure, Mark washed sand only for a moment before artifacts appeared: chairs, a bed with a mattress of horse hair, a wooden crate containing 12 pairs of boots, and a stack of wooden floor joists for two ready-to-build homes (prefab). Our research indicated the *Arabia* had been carrying the makings for two homes in Logan, Nebraska. The size of lumber showed the houses would have measured only 16 by 20 feet; not big by modern standards.

The wash water also exposed a small wooden trunk trimmed with one-half inch metal strips and decorated with brass tacks. We all gathered around, eager to see inside. Acting like two excited children, Jerry and I carefully lifted the lid. Inside lay a tattered black wool felt hat with a large piece in the shape of a horse shoe missing from its brim. The box obviously contained personal belongings, my favorite type of discovery. Gently lifting up the hat for our families and friends to see, I jokingly commented that the missing piece from the brim may have been the result of an angry horse. Beneath the hat and a thin layer of mud lay a pair of pants with a checkered green and brown pattern. The pants were short, turned inside out, and had a cloth patch sewn on both knees. Moving deeper into the chest we found a muddy pair of boots with badly worn soles. The angle of wear and the severity of their condition indicated the man who owned these boots was extremely bow-legged. Below the footwear were two brown jugs, one empty and

Whether posing for a photo or working in the mud, Greg's children, Kristin (left), and Derek, enjoyed spending time at the excavation.

Photos by Karen Hawley

These supplies were as essential to the pioneers as tires are to modern travelers.
Photo by Greg Hawley

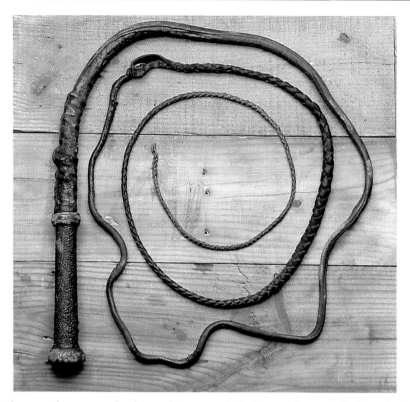

Early manufactures made these whips out of flexible rubber and braided leather.
Photo by Greg Hawley

the other two-thirds full of liquor. Underneath the jugs we found a small coin purse holding three coins: two dimes dated 1843 and 1832, and one half-dime dated 1853, for a total of 25 cents.

We continued washing away sand until another box came into view. Horse tack filled the box: bits, stirrups, spurs, bridles, a pulling harness, reins, buggy whips, and 12 bullwhips measuring 12 feet in length. The first seven feet of the bull whip, including the handle, were soft flexible rubber, and the five remaining feet were braided leather tapering down at the end. I was surprised to discover rubber whips had snapped over the heads of horses and oxen in 1856!

The day's final discovery was a crate containing an array of personal belongings: a tin whale oil lamp, one skillet, two tin coffee pots, a salt shaker, two iron kettles, a spice rack with bottles, 13 clothes pins, a

Found on the main deck of the Arabia, *these items belonged to a deck passenger. Deck passengers supplied their own food and drink, slept on the cold floor and endured the noise of hissing steam and thundering engines.*   Photo by Greg Hawley water dipper, two fluted pie plates, three cooking pans, a rolling pin, an ax handle, one pair of shoes, one padlock, one door lock, a griddle, an ink bottle, one hammer head, matches, a wooden bucket, a tin bucket, three clothing irons, one iron holder, four stove legs, two ironstone pitchers, four tin cups, and one spittoon.

As I drove home that night, I thought about the owner of that wooden box decorated with brass tacks. The items told a tale of a poor, short, bow-legged man. A man who fancied a jug of liquor as a traveling companion, had 25 cents to sustain his monetary needs, and occasionally wore a hat that suggested a brief encounter with an angry horse.

What fortitude he must have had to strike westward with such meager belongings. Perhaps he was running from his past or, like so

left *These personal belongings tell a story of a poor man with humble belongings.*

Photo by Greg Hawley

The only thing better than finding buried treasure is finding it with family and friends.
Photo by Florence Hawley

many others, was motivated by dreams of a better life. Though I will never know his identity, I found it a privilege to have met this man through the items most precious in his life.

Fighting the Sand
December 19, 1988

With the weekend gone, so were the volunteers. Only Jerry, Mom, Dad, Dave, and I showed up to dig. The wind whipped across the excavation's opening, churning up a swirling blizzard of sand. Even with goggles for protection, I constantly had to rub the sand from my eyes, brush it from my hair, and spit it from my mouth.

Despite the blowing sand, we completed the wiring and piping of the fourteenth and fifteenth wells, increasing our de-watering capacity from 13,000 gallons to 15,000 gallons of water per minute.

The Salvage of 1897
December 20, 1988

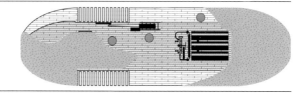

Tuesday, December 20, brought good news. Overnight the water table dropped five inches. Not a huge amount, but it was progress.

We continued to work on the piping and wiring of pumps and generators. By late afternoon, the need to make a discovery was unbearable.

Washing the *Arabia*'s deck, I noticed the sand suddenly appeared marble-like and rolled across the exposed planking. I shut off the water and knelt for a closer look. It was not sand rolling away but lead shot in a variety of sizes. I saw no container. Perhaps a cotton sack long since dissolved left the lead to mix in with the sand. I scooped up the sand inside a ten-foot circle into buckets and decided to separate out the lead later.

The *Arabia*'s timbers were held in place by pegs, bolts, long boat builders' spikes, and thousands of square nails. I was surprised to find large numbers of modern-style round nails hammered into two six-foot circles of planks on the steamer's main deck. Then I remembered "Dad" Henson's salvage attempt of 1897. The circles mark the point of entry of Henson's salvage.

The removal of additional sand revealed more evidence of Henson's salvage. Sitting just ahead of the larboard engine and adjacent to the boilers was a six-foot diameter steel tube, four feet in height with handles on the inside. This tube represented the lower section of the caisson used to reach the *Arabia*. Laying beneath the tube was a third hole: Henson's final attempt to find whiskey aboard the *Arabia*.

As I knelt and closely inspected the remains of Henson's salvage efforts, I wondered how successful he really was. Nightfall was approaching, and there was not enough time to look below the deck. We would have to wait for tomorrow and hope that "Dad" left something behind for us.

The Salvage of 1897

The *Kansas City Star*, dated June 1910, and George B. Merrick's *Steamboats and Steamboatmen of the Upper Mississippi* reported details of the 1897 salvage. This chapter in the *Arabia*'s history began in a saloon in Holt, Missouri. One night, the mayor of Holt, Gale "Dad" Henson, was having a few drinks when an old man sitting at a table nearby began to share the story of the *Arabia* and its treasure of lost whiskey. This old-timer instilled treasure hunting fever in Dad Henson, and he wasted little time bringing his friends together and forming a salvage company called the Holt Syndicate.

To dig the *Arabia* one must first find it, and as Henson and his team soon discovered, finding it was not easy. The land had changed in appearance since the first salvage attempt in 1877. The river had shifted further to the northeast, and willow thickets covered much of the area. To find the *Arabia*, Henson's group first consulted soothsayers—seventh sons of seventh sons—but with all their prophetic power they could not locate the steamer.

According to newspaper accounts, the use of mystical power by one soothsayer had merit. "A survivor of the wreck is living in the person of C.A. Carside, but as he was only six months old, he is not able to help the sanguine searchers with the recollections of the affair."

The Holt Syndicate then hired masters of the divining rod, but they too failed to find the lost steamer.

Henson and his band were not easily deterred. Hoping to hit the *Arabia*, they drove steel probe rods 30 feet into the ground. They pushed through willow thickets and waded swamps, searching 160 acres without success. The back-breaking work often drew a crowd from nearby communities and farms. Everyone had an opinion on where the *Arabia* lay hidden.

George Summers, a local farmer, worked a track of land on the Missouri side, just opposite where the *Arabia* sank. Summers observed the Henson's exploration efforts for many days and more than once poked fun at their efforts and methods.

"You find it if you know so much," Dad Henson declared.

Summers replied, "Well, I'll just do that. After all, the *Arabia* went down across the river from my farm. And if I didn't see the *Arabia* sink, then my name is not George Summers."

Henson's jaw dropped. "Why didn't you tell us in the first place?"

"You never asked me," Summers replied.

George Summers did not share a single clue to the whereabouts of the *Arabia* until Henson and the Holt Syndicate agreed to make him an equal partner in the venture.

To find the *Arabia*, Summers insisted that Henson cross the river to his farm on the Missouri side. Skeptically, Henson and his party loaded into Summers' leaky boat and rowed to the far bank. When they arrived, Summers harnessed a mare and walked her to the edge of the farm. Acting as if he was plowing his field, Summers swung the horse down the turning row of his field and stopped.

With a crooked finger and swollen knuckle, he pointed between the ears of the mare and announced, "There she is." He explained that after the *Arabia* sank, her tall smoke stacks continued to rise high above the water until floating ice tore them down the following winter. Each time he plowed along his turning row, the stacks of the *Arabia* lined up perfectly between the ears of his horse.

Using the directional bearings provided by old man Summers, Henson and the Holt Syndicate went back across the river. They resumed probing with long rods and soon found the *Arabia*.

To overcome the groundwater, the Holt Syndicate constructed a steel tube, or caisson, six-feet in diameter and over 30-feet in height. They designed the caisson with two separate air-tight compartments, one chamber above the other. With two men inside the tube digging out sand and dirt, the caisson's weight slowly settled into the ground.

When they encountered the water table, Henson pumped compressed air into the caisson forcing the groundwater down and out of the steel tube. The workers could remove sand without the loss of pressure by passing the soil up into the second compartment before closing the air-tight door that separated the two chambers. By equalizing the pressure in the upper chamber, workers outside the caisson removed the sand, then repressurized the chamber to await the next ascending load.

The working environment within the caisson was horrific. Less than one man in ten could withstand the confinement, noise, heat, and excruciating pressure on the ear drums.

On December 8, 1897, thirty days after breaking ground over the *Arabia*, Henson and his partners reached the main deck of the steamboat. It was critical that the caisson fit tightly to the steamer's pine deck. Henson's objective was to pressurize not only the caisson, but also the cargo hold of the *Arabia*. Digging into the *Arabia* like miners into a mountain side, these early salvagers claimed to recover a barrel of pork, running gear for a wagon, lumber, hats, and chamber pots. Over the course of 90 days they sank the caisson three times on the *Arabia's* main deck. With not one drop of whiskey found, the salvagers abandoned the excavation.

The Holt Syndicate used a caisson during their salvage attempt on the Arabia *in 1897.*
Illustrations by Jim Murray

Boot and Shoe Rich
December 21, 1988

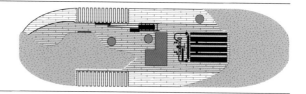

I spent the early hours of Wednesday, December 21, rolling over in my bed and gazing at my alarm clock, wondering if morning would ever come. Today we were to remove planking next to Dad Henson's salvage efforts.

By 10:00 A.M., my partners and I were organized and ready for action. Forcing a crow bar between the pine decking, my father leaned hard and leveraged free the first plank; it squeaked defiantly. Dad continued on to the next board, and Jerry, Dave, and I joined in. Within a few minutes we removed several boards, revealing a cargo bay brimming with grayish black river mud. Builders of the *Arabia* hammered the pine decking into place so precisely during construction that sand did not pass between the boards and into the cargo bay. Over time river silt seeped in where the sand could not, filling the cargo hold with a sticky quagmire of sour-smelling mud we soon learned to hate.

We aimed our wash hoses into the exposed cavity and increased the water pressure, expecting the mud to boil from the cargo hold. It did not. The river mud was thick like clay; and the water ricocheted back, drenching us with a dirty spray.

With hand shovels and water hoses, we slowly moved downward through the thick mud. Wooden boxes poked through the mud everywhere. I knelt and carefully pried open the closest box. It was full of boots. The next box was full of shoes.

"Shoes!" my Dad exclaimed, after prying open two more boxes.

"Boots," Jerry declared. All the exposed boxes, 20 crates in all, contained foot apparel.

My enthusiasm crushed, I suddenly felt tired and sat down. My partners did the same. Caked in cold river mud, we looked more like the losers of a mud wrestling competition than treasure hunters. We yearned for gold and silver, not the world's largest collection of muddy boots and shoes.

"Boot and shoe rich," I said to myself, driving home late that night

Approximately 5,000 boots and shoes fell victim to the Missouri River when the Arabia *sank. They remain in remarkable condition, except for cotton thread long since dissolved from stitched seams. Excavators estimate that hand sewing and chemically preserving this footwear will take 25 years.*   Photo by Greg Hawley

right *The crushing weight of sand on top of the steamer collapsed the center section of the* Arabia's *hull. Large numbers of boots, shoes, and other artifacts found in this area sustained damages.*
Photo by Dave Hawley

with a truck load of wet and muddy footwear. I was trying to be optimistic. After all, not everything discovered aboard the *Arabia* could be golden treasure. We had worked for months, investing time, money, heart, and soul into this project. And we had gotten back, well... plenty of "soles."

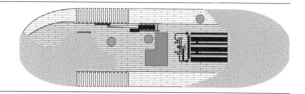

We wanted to bring the sixteenth well on-line before the weather turned bad. Installing de-watering wells was now less than exciting, especially with the *Arabia*'s decking partially removed and boxes exposed.

Since the dig began, I had noticed an increase in my daily consumption of food. The calories necessary to work 18-hour days in

left *Mark Scherer and friend Chris Davis remove a wagon wheel from the excavation site.*

Photo by Bob Hawley

right *The river's force damaged the steamer, but amid the destruction this fragile bottle of wine remained intact.*

Photo by Greg Hawley

freezing weather were enormous. After eating a big breakfast, Jerry brought in food from his restaurant for lunch. Leaning against the *Arabia's* steam engine or sitting on her deck, we stuffed ourselves with cheeseburgers, fries, and soft drinks before resuming our work.

The water table had dropped an additional six-inches overnight, allowing us to engage the lowest point of the *Arabia's* main deck.

Next to the starboard paddle wheel, we discovered two wagon wheels, two axles, lumber, broken chairs, two circular saws, a crate containing two window sashes, 12 window panes per sash, a shattered lantern, and a bottle of wine. Surrounded by woven wicker, the bottle's cork remained firmly in place.

Christmas Eve
December 24, 1988

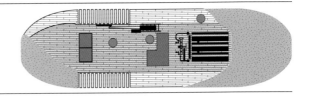

I was first to arrive at the dig and immediately checked the water table. The sixteenth well had removed an additional 12 inches overnight. Still, the water continued to defy us. Pouring through the sand and into the excavation site at 40 feet below ground level, the water level remained five feet too high. We needed more pumps, which meant it was time to revisit the banker.

As the work began, we tried not to dwell on our financial problems. How would we ever pay for this over-budgeted and unaffordable adventure?

The *Arabia* seemed to sense our frustration. Each time we showed a reluctance to continue the digging, the steamer teased us with exciting discoveries. Next to the starboard wheel, Jerry uncovered a wooden crate containing four black wool felt hats. The hats were tall with wide brims and were in amazingly good shape.

Near the hats, I uncovered a box revealing items that belonged to a female traveler. The box held a rotating silver spice rack with bottles containing nutmeg, peppercorn, cloves, a bottle of sarsaparilla manufactured in New York, 12 white plates manufactured by Wedgwood, with matching cups, and a bow saw. The bow saw seemed out of place, and I wondered why it was there.

We also found eight cast iron kettles and two block and tackles for hoisting cargo. Nearby, the boat's "capstan," once used for pulling the steamer off sandbars and snags, or cinching up to port, protruded upward. Forward of the capstan we exposed the *Arabia's* cargo hatch. By this time it was late, and we were tired. We peeked into the open hatch before shutting down for the night. The hatch was full of boxes for another day.

It was dark when I loaded the last of the day's treasure into my pickup truck. As I drove home I realized it was Christmas Eve. For the first time I hadn't helped my wife decorate the Christmas tree and hang stockings

Six years after the 1988 excavation, a lab technician cleaning a snatch block discovered the word Arabia *stamped into the wood.*

Photos by Greg Hawley

The treasures found on Christmas Eve could not compensate excavators for the precious time away from their families.   **Photo by Bob Hawley**

on the mantel. My children, by now fast asleep, had already listened to the Christmas story read by their mother, not me. I felt a sense of isolation and loneliness as I passed brightly lit homes. I had found some treasure, but I had lost this Christmas Eve.

Home for Christmas
December 25, 1988

After many days fighting water, mud, and the elements of winter, I took the whole day off.

"It's nice to have you home," my wife said. I enjoyed watching three-year-old Kristin and four-year-old Derek tear into their presents. It was a cherished moment of sanity amidst chaos. After our children had opened their presents, my wife and I agreed the ultimate treasure was already in our possession: a loving family.

CHAPTER 7

Entering
the Stern

A Ribbon of Gold
December 26, 1988

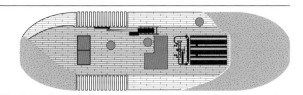

A s I opened my eyes, I heard water running down the gutters of my home and a cold wind slapping rain against the house.

To endure the harsh elements of winter, combined with blowing sand, sloppy mud, and the spray from our wash hoses, our team adorned ourselves with apparel fitting for the occasion: long underwear, two pairs of wool socks, insulated overalls, chest-waders, a raincoat with a hood, shoulder-length rubber gloves, and eye goggles.

Completely dressed, I was ready for just about anything, except wiping my nose. As soon as I stepped into the dig, I was covered with mud. I found myself in one of those frustrating moments, with my face splattered and dripping with slimy muck. My gloves were so slimy and difficult to remove, it was not practical to wipe my face. The only clean spot for perhaps a mile around was right in the middle of Jerry's back. I knew better than to ask permission. I just grabbed both his shoulders and wiped away.

"What are you doing?" Jerry said, turning towards me. I simply smiled, shook his hand, and walked away.

We tried to ignore the cold howling wind, rain, and freezing drizzle. Dad and I began the day by digging through the stern's open cargo hatch. Dave, Jerry, and some friends maintained water pumps, hoses, and helped lift mud out of the hole. The first crate directly beneath the open cargo hatch contained 40 boxes of cigars. The cigars held their shape well and still smelled of tobacco.

We worked our way beneath the deck and deeper into the cargo bay.

Excavators found thousands of cigars, boxes of chewing tobacco, and clay pipes aboard the Arabia.   **Photo by Greg Hawley**

After a few minutes of additional washing, a large box measuring three and one-half feet wide, three feet deep and three feet tall, took shape. We removed the mud that surrounded the box with gloved hands, placed the goo into buckets, and passed it back and up through the cargo hatch like an old-fashioned fire brigade. One hour later, Dad and I knelt beside the box, lifted the lid, and gently sprayed water inside.

"It has saddles inside," Dad yelled upward. Two of the saddles had horns, two without. Lifting them from the box, we passed them topside to our excited partners and friends. The box also held 12 brass bits, two bridles, and decorative brass buttons stamped with a figure of a horse head.

Dad and I eagerly eyed another large box located deep in the cargo hold. Like two moles, we tunneled our way toward it.

As we dug, I glanced at Dad's muddy appearance and wondered if I looked as bad as he did. Dirty water ran down his face and dripped from his nose, whiskers, and chin. His hot breath created a white cloud of exhaust in the cold cavity that pulsed with the rhythm of his digging.

"At least we're out of the rain," Dad joked, as we dug through the

Greg prepares to tunnel toward an unopened box located far beneath the deck.
Photo by Dave Hawley

slime. On hands and knees we worked closer and closer to our goal.

"Let's stop for the night," Jerry called.

I turned to Dad. "I don't know about you, but I'm not leaving this hole until I see what's in that box." Dad agreed. Within minutes, I was prying open the crate.

"Pass down the light and water hose," I called.

Dad slid in beside me—we could barely fit together in the crevasse—and shot water into the box. A ribbon of gold glistened back at us; the box contained dishes trimmed in gold.

Our confinement prevented us from jumping up and down, so we just lay in the mud, shoulder to shoulder, speaking quickly in whispers, not willing to lose or share the moment.

"What ya find?" an anxious voice called from above.

"Not much," Dad hollered back. "You can all go home. I know you're tired. Greg and I will finish up tonight." Dad and I savored our position of power over our helpless partners and friends above deck. The suspense was killing them, and we loved every moment.

Eventually, we handed up the first of many gold-rimmed dishes. The formerly impatient support team was now chanting oo's and ah's as they gazed upon each new treasure.

The dishes were stunning: a serving bowl with golden handles in the shape of a ram's head, cups with no handles, saucers, dishes, a teapot trimmed in gold, fancy drinking glasses with amber tint, four glass salt dips, a syrup pitcher with lid, a clear glass bowl, and one candle holder.

"It can't get any better," I thought. Yet it did. In the bottom of the box, I glimpsed a beautiful white pitcher. Dad and I held our breath as we washed away the mud, hoping the jug was intact. I pulled it up gently while Dad helped to dislodge it with a soft spray of water. The ivory porcelain jug depicted a tropical setting of palm trees and beaches. One side profiled two young children, one holding the other, and on the opposite side, an elegant woman stood next to a man.

Lying in the bowels of the *Arabia*, our bodies matted with mud and half frozen with cold, we could think of no place on earth we would rather be.

Since finding the white pitcher, we have sought to discover the story behind this exquisite piece. In 1788, the novel *Paul and Virginia*, by Bernardin de St. Pierre was published in France. By 1802, the book reached its sixth edition, receiving world-wide acclaim. The novel so impressed Napoleon Bonaparte that he decorated and granted a pension to St. Pierre.

The novel tells a story of two young and fatherless children raised together in France. They eventually fell deeply in love, but during a sea voyage a raging storm blew the ship against jagged rocks off the coast. Paul tried to reach Virginia, but the storm forced him back. He watched from shore as a naked sailor tried to persuade Virginia to cast off her heavy clothing so she could swim safely to land. Thinking more of her dignity than her life, she refused and drowned when the ship sank. Paul died of a broken heart two months later.

According to information in *Relief-Molded Jugs 1820-1900*, by R. K. Henrywood, many experts believe, despite the lack of conclusive evidence, the wide-spread popularity of this novel inspired Thomas John and Joseph Mayer—well known in the Staffordshire Potteries—to produce this raised-relief jug made of parian (porcelain).

Through the passing of centuries, the jug has received the title "Family."

Made in England, this raised-relief jug represents a passengers desire for finery on the frontier.
Photos by Greg Hawley

The gold-rimmed china undoubtedly belonged to a wealthy passenger aboard the Arabia. *Although no markings are visible, the dishes resemble French chinaware produced by Haviland.*
Photo by Greg Hawley

Black and White In Color
December 27, 1988

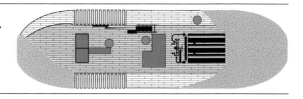

It had poured all night, and I wondered how much sand had eroded from the banks of the excavation and back into the hole. When I arrived at the site I could not believe what I saw. Our 100-ton crane was teetering precariously on the lip of the excavation, the heavy rain had washed away the sand from beneath its tracks. It was a real cliff hanger as we inched it backwards to safety. If the crane had fallen, the damage to the *Arabia*, combined with the cost of removing the crane, might have finished us financially.

Partners and wives resumed our now ritualistic search for treasure. We removed pine decking over the cargo hold where we had discovered the gold-rimmed dishware, saddles, and cigars. Within the hour we exposed the largest box we had discovered thus far. My father removed the lid and slid his hand gently through the mud, but he felt nothing. When he took out his hand, bright blue mud covered his glove. Dad pushed his hand deeper into the box revealing a rainbow of yellow, red, orange, and green mud. Completely bewildered by this colorful tapestry, Dad dug deeper and made the first tangible discovery: a stack of six long-sleeve red shirts made of wool, the top one covered with dozens of unattached white buttons. Many of the clothes were apparently cotton, long since dissolved, leaving behind only colored dyes as a testimony to their vibrant colors. The crate's remaining contents revealed double-breasted brown, black, and green coats with wooden buttons; brown checkered pants with a button-up fly; additional red shirts; and hundreds of loose buttons.

I picked up a green wool coat and studied it. During my research I had reviewed hundreds of photographs of people, ranging from very rich to the unfortunate poor. The clothing was represented in shades of black and white, daguerreotype imagery of the times. To see this vibrant clothing made me realize the pioneers of 1856 were, as we are today, brightly fashionable, not drab and conservative.

Cradling a red shirt in my hand, I felt the decades that separated the

Buttons found aboard the Arabia *number in the tens of thousands. Their beauty is as diverse as their compositions, and include wood, rubber, glass, horn, brass, china, and steel.*
Photo by Greg Hawley

Excavators found the clothing and material aboard the Arabia *brightly fashionable. The material's composition was primarily that of protein: beaver hair, wool, and silk.*
Photo by Greg Hawley

present from the past narrow considerably.

According to *Folkwear*, "Patterns from Times Past," the red shirts were in the style of "Missouri River Boatman." Used by fur traders, fishermen, rowdies, raftmen, and even gentlemen, these shirts were popular during the mid-1800s. George Caleb Bingham (1811-1879) often used this style of shirt in his paintings.

The day ended with the discovery of several cooking stoves and a box containing a host of new merchandise, ranging from tableware to tools, from sewing supplies to pencils.

Leaving the *Arabia*, our hopes were running high. Unfortunately, so was the cost of digging this boat. The water table remained above most of the cargo. We had little choice but to buy more pumps, pipe, wire, control boxes, fuel, and one more generator.

International Freight
December 28, 1988

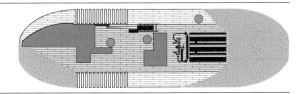

I woke up late. The long days had finally caught up with me. There was no need for a time clock on this project. Everyone was working as hard as they could. As Mark Twain said once, we were "working from can to cain't."

We decided to remove decking from the larboard side of the *Arabia*, from the stern forward to the paddle wheel. The starboard side, due to the tilting of the boat, continued to lie unattainably beneath the water table.

As the day's work progressed, the *Arabia*'s appearance changed dramatically. The exposed floor joists resembled the ribs of an ancient dinosaur. Considering her precise construction, it seemed unfair to alter her so quickly. We felt we should delve into the *Arabia* like a wine connoisseur slowly drinking the last remaining bottle from a great year, savoring each precious drop. However, the *Arabia*'s cargo was now exposed to oxygen, and vulnerable to rapid deterioration. With the skyrocketing cost of digging, we had to move ahead quickly.

My partners and I were edgy and short tempered from too many long hours and too much money spent. It's a good thing our hands were always slippery with mud; it made getting a good grip around each others' necks difficult.

By early afternoon we had removed a large expanse of deck and turned our attention to finding artifacts. We worked in teams for better efficiency. In the cargo hold, we often sank in mud above our knees, and moving around was a joint effort. To free ourselves we shoved the wash hose nozzle into mud next to our legs and blasted away. At times it seemed easier to free the boxes than each other.

Since the dig had begun, our team felt confident we were digging the *Arabia*, but with so many steamers sinking on the Missouri we were continually looking for conclusive proof. Because the river washed away the upper decks, any sign displaying the name *Arabia* was somewhere downriver. We had to look for other clues.

With the removal of deck planking from the stern we discovered the *Arabia's* tiller arm. The tiller arm attaches to the rudder and was necessary to steer the boat. It's discovery was conclusive evidence that we had found the *Arabia*. Research before the excavation indicated the *Arabia* had run aground near Jefferson City. The accident broke the tiller arm, and the captain ordered men to replace it with a straight tree cut from along the shore. The tiller arm we discovered was the same tree. It still had some bark attached, and the end remained tapered from the ax. It was conclusive proof that we had indeed found the *Arabia*.

Not far from the tiller arm was a small keg of cheese in excellent shape, but not so excellent that I cared to try it. A wooden crate contained chewing tobacco wrapped in lead foil. Two large boxes held a variety of textiles: coats, shirts, socks, skeins of yarn, bolts of wool, and a new discovery, silk. Coal black, the silk appeared unblemished and strong.

Pioneers viewed silk with high regard during the mid-1800s, as this July 17, 1843, article in the St. Louis, *Missouri Republican* illustrates:

> **Silk Dresses** — Silk being a nonconductor of electricity, is an excellent material for dress. One of the primary causes of the languor which is felt in damp weather is said to be the damp atmosphere robbing us of our electricity, which a medical writer calls the buoyant cordial of the body.

Greg Hawley removes the remains of a bolt of material. Long strands of red silk survived, but the cross weave made of cotton dissolved.
Photo by Dave Hawley

Those, therefore who are apt to be spiritless in damp weather are recommended to wear silk waistcoats, drawers, and stockings. Silk should be used in every possible manner by the weak—in the lining of the sleeves, cloaks, coverlets, & c.

The next box read, "T and P, Logan, Family Soap." Inside the crate, a cube of brownish goo was partially dissolved and crystallized.

Logan, Nebraska, was located just across and upriver from Sioux City, Iowa. Logan, Nebraska, undoubtedly suffered during the winter of 1856, having lost 740 boxes of freight and two prefab homes when the *Arabia* sank. Today, all that remains of Logan, Nebraska, is at the Arabia Steamboat Museum.

All that remains of merchants T and P (Tracy and Papin) and Logan, Nebraska, sits in the Arabia Steamboat Museum.   **Photo by Greg Hawley**

Next, we found a box containing 12 bottles of brandied cherries with the corks firmly in place. Packed in straw, the bright red cherries looked as if someone had bottled them only yesterday.

The writing on the box was in French, indicating their journey had been a long one. The cherries came first by steamship to New York, then by train to St. Louis, Missouri, and finally by steamboat to the frontier. Merchants sold the cherries for a costly $1.50 a bottle retail, and had them delivered over 6,000 miles by sea, land, and river, just so their customers could make cherry pies.

A narrow box labeled "I.W. Matthew Co. Milling, Thomas and Farkin, St. Louis," contained wooden carpenter levels. I lifted one against the sun's light and observed a tiny bubble of 1850s air trapped in the leveling glass. Nearby were two stacks of wooden buckets—12 per stack—and a stack of wooden washtubs in progressive sizes. We discovered a bundle of 12 brooms, a stack of 12 shovels, and a box containing six washboards. A small box contained one-pound cans of "Fresh Cove Oysters" from Baltimore, clearly labeled and smelling terrible. A larger box contained black, green, and brown wool frock coats with wooden and rubber buttons. Unfortunately, the cotton thread holding the garments together had long since dissolved. To repair these coats, we would have to hand sew the cuffs, sleeves, buttons, collars, and pockets back together.

With pickup trucks heaped full of old cargo boxes, we left the dig site. On the way home, highway commuters looked at us with bewilderment. Our convoy appeared paradoxical. An 1856 wagon train of cargo had merged with twentieth-century technology and was speeding down the highway at 70 miles per hour.

Brandied cherries traveled over 6,000 miles from France so pioneers could make cherry pies.
Photo by Greg Hawley

A Hardship for the Family
December 29, 1988

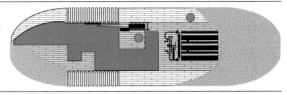

I awoke with the familiar sound of the clothes dryer tumbling my excavation apparel around and around. For weeks, Karen had taken on the unpleasant task of making sure my clothing was dry and clean for the following day. By the time I got home, every pocket and seam in my work clothing was full of river sand. Tumbling out in the washing machine and clothes dryer, it mixed in with my family's life: bedspreads, pajamas, socks, and underwear. I was afraid that divorce was as close as one more load of sandy clothes.

When I arrived at the dig, my father was noticeably absent. He was out fixing a furnace. Although our refrigeration, heating, and cooling business was slower during the winter, customers continued to call for help. Dad refused to install new equipment for anyone while we were digging the boat. It would have taken us away from the dig for too long. Dad, Dave, and I ran a few service calls, but only late at night or first thing in the morning. Long-time customers were growing impatient and beginning to call other companies. We feared these same customers might never call back. Invariably, we would measure the cost of digging the *Arabia* for years to come.

When Dad arrived, we began removing decking between the paddle wheels on both the larboard and starboard sides. To save time, we split into two work parties. Instantly, we discovered three cast iron cooking stoves, but only one was strong enough to remove intact.

Beside the stoves, we found a long narrow box containing 24 yellow stoneware canning jars. Accompanying tin lids displayed a brass label stamped with the words "R. Arthur, Patent, Jan. 2, 1855." The user filled the jar with fruits or vegetables, then pushed the vertical edge of the lid down into the wax-filled groove, which created an airtight seal.

Next to the canning jars was a box containing irons for clothing. Ironing generally took place in the morning, while the cooking stove was still hot from breakfast. Since one iron was never enough, they were

These self-sealing yellow stoneware canning jars represented cutting edge technology in the mid-1800s.
Photo by Greg Hawley

commonly sold in sets of three.

Moving on through the mud and muck, we discovered three black cooking skillets with long handles, a stack of 12 shovels, suspenders, 17 pairs of black stockings, bias tape, metal spigots for wooden barrels, kegs of salted pork, cheese, a burlap sack of half-inch rope, 48 ax heads, spoons, forks, knives, boots, lumber, saw blades, 12 cast iron trays, wood tools, bolts of cloth, kettles, tobacco, and dozens of pocket knives in remarkably good condition.

After unloading a truckload of treasure, I returned home and quickly shed my muddy clothing, showered, and slipped between the covers. Karen, long since asleep, lay quietly beside me. I set the alarm clock for 5:00 A.M. and cringed at the current time: 12:43 A.M. Yet, even as I was drifting off, I wondered what new treasures awaited us.

A Keg of Booze
December 30, 1988

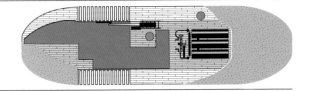

The day began with cloudy skies and temperatures in the low 20s. Although I was anxious to begin digging, I needed to care for previously discovered artifacts. Leather items needed freezing, wooden artifacts needed moistening, and the recently discovered brandied cherries needed wax applied to the corks to help seal out bacteria.

When I finally arrived at the excavation, my partners were washing sand from the starboard side of the *Arabia* near the paddle wheel. The work went slowly, with much of the *Arabia* still below the water table. Previous core samples taken from this area produced broken red goblets with gold etching. We hoped that large quantities of expensive red glassware were hidden beneath the deck.

With the deck planks removed and the washing underway, we soon uncovered the box marked by our initial core sample. The box contained a magnificent candelabra made of bronze and eloquently adorned with grapes, leaves, and vines. Moving deeper into the box, we were sickened by what we saw. Two hand-painted glass figurines, one of a man, the other a woman, were shattered. The churning drill bit from our core sample had broken them both. Scattered about were remnants of four red and four clear goblets.

"If we had drilled one foot in any direction, we would have missed this box," Dad reminded us. "Without red glass in the core sample, we may not have dug the *Arabia*."

Next, we found a box containing handheld coffee grinders and a small wooden keg with a corn cob sticking out of the top. Hickory hoops encircled the small keg, but water had weakened them. As we removed the mud, the wooden hoops fell into small pieces, and the staves separated. A black sticky paste oozed out. Gathering up the leaking muck, we decided it was pine tar. Pioneers applied pine tar to open wounds on both livestock and people to help prevent infections.

As Dad and I pried another barrel from beneath two floor joists, I heard a sloshing sound. "Ale" was written on the lid. A keg of beer was

A core sample taken from the Arabia *verified the presence of cargo, but damaged these precious items.*
Photo by Greg Hawley

a far cry from the 400 barrels of Kentucky Bourbon reported on board in 1856.

Later that night, after unloading the day's discoveries at the lab, Dad and I went on to his house with the keg of ale. We were curious. Dad laid the keg on its side and used a toothpick size drill bit to bore a hole through an oak stave. Tipping the barrel over a small cup, the fluid dribbled out. From the smell and appearance, river water had seeped in and ruined the ale.

**A Fragrance
From the Past
December 31, 1988**

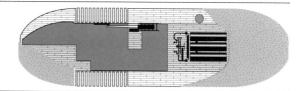

I was running behind schedule and I worried my partners might start without me. I much preferred making discoveries, not hearing about them.

I slid down the embankment of the excavation before they opened the first box.

"This is like Christmas everyday," Jerry said.

No one disagreed. Adrenaline flooded our veins with each discovery. We had stepped from reality into a fantasy world. I would be a millionaire if I could only bottle and sell this sensation.

The boxes brimmed with new merchandise destined for a general store. The treasures ranged from golden jewelry, fragrant lotions smelling of coconut, and perfume, to black powder flasks, bleeding knives, glass trade beads, and more. Each item has its own intriguing history.

Early fur trappers and traders used trade goods to barter for animal pelts, food, lodging, and other essentials. The most popular trade item was beads. Indians used them to adorn their clothing and leather apparel.

The smallest and most numerous beads discovered on the *Arabia* were seed beads. According to information in *A Bead Primer*, by

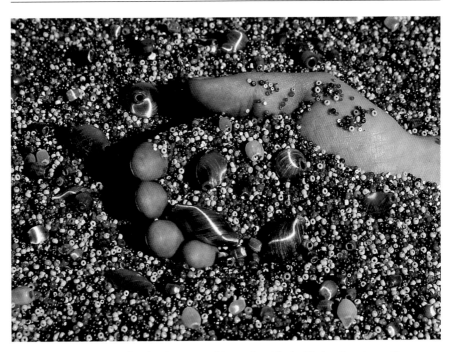

These tiny treasures are glass beads once used in trade with the Native Americans. Excavators found an estimated five million beads in a variety of colors and sizes.   **Photo by Greg Hawley**

Elizabeth Harris, they were probably manufactured in Venice, Italy, or Bohemia. To manufacture these beads, artisans melted glass into a molten mixture. Then the bead maker gathered the molten glass on the end of his blow pipe and blew in a bubble of air. A second workman attached a pulling rod to the opposite end of the molten bubble and both men walked, or sometimes ran, in opposite directions. The glowing mass stretched into a cooling wisp of glass with a very long bubble inside. Workers then cut the drawn tube of glass into meter lengths and again into small, jagged-edged beads. They placed the beads in metal drums with sand and ash, and rotated the drums over a hot fire. The ash filled the hole in the beads, giving them support, while the sand and heat smoothed out the jagged edges. Placing the now rounded beads in bags, workers shook them from side to side for polishing. Finally, young women prepared the beads for shipment by stringing them on cotton thread.

The bleeding knives had three blades, each one a different size. When pioneers got sick they often visited their local barber for help. He used a bleeding knife to cut the flesh and drain out "bad blood." People thought that if they removed the sick blood, good blood would replace it. The striped barber pole in front of modern barber shops remains a symbol of this once common practice. The red stripe represents blood, and the white stripe bandages.

The perfume was golden in color and the bottles decorative and graceful. We removed the stoppers from two dissimilar bottles and inhaled a tapestry of floral aromas. One hundred and thirty-two years beneath the water, mud, and sand, yet the fragrance continued to permeate. My partners and I paused to adorn ourselves. A dab on the wrist for some, for others a light touch to the neck. Covered with mud and dressed in chest waders, raincoats, and rubber gloves, we looked out of place for such an occasion. However, experiencing the past through the sense of smell made this moment one I will never forget. After all, men and women both used perfume in the 1800s. Besides, how many times in my life would I get to smell like a pioneer?

This perfume had come from France and is perhaps the oldest in the world still retaining its original fragrance. Cool temperatures, darkness, and the absence of oxygen protected the fragrance. Because of the perfume's pristine condition, technicians at IFF, International Flavors

Cool temperatures, darkness, and the absence of oxygen preserved the French perfume found aboard the steamboat Arabia.   **Photo by Greg Hawley**

and Fragrances Inc., located in New York City, were able to analyze the perfumes and discover their ingredients. One fragrance contained aldehydes, mimosa, marigold, jasmine, muguet, rose, narcissi, moss, vetivert, sandalwood, musk, and orris. With IFF's help, our families reproduced this bouquet of scent. Though the original name will probably remain a mystery, its aroma will live forever.

**Weapons Found
January 1, 1989**

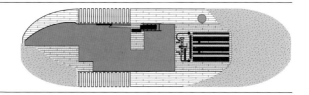

Rising from bed well before dawn, I thought first of the *Arabia*. Then I remembered my truck sitting in the garage, still brimming over with cargo from the previous day. I hurried to the lab and unloaded my truck, cleaned and dried metals, wet down leather and wood, and froze textiles.

Our preservation lab seemed to become smaller as the quantity of artifacts grew. Boxes of doorknobs, locks, keys, and dishes reached to the ceiling. The walk-in cooler and freezer were crowded with textiles, leather, and food products. With less than half the *Arabia* salvaged, I could barely squeeze in the door. It was time to deliver wooden artifacts to our underground storage facility. To accommodate these materials, we bought ten 1,000-gallon capacity livestock watering tanks. These water-filled tanks provided a stable environment for the wood until we could begin preservation.

When I arrived at the dig, my partners greeted me with the story of a new discovery: two large bundles of cowhides. We estimated the water-soaked hides weighed 500 pounds. Since they were too heavy to lift all at once, we peeled the hides off individually. The hides were marked with the cattleman's brand, the square footage, and the tanner, L. NORTHRUP, HARPERSVILLE, NY. When butchering these animals, they had sliced them from head to tail, right down the middle.

Three hundred cow hides later, we moved ahead with hoses and shovels in search of more treasure. My father loosened the lid on a long narrow box and looked inside.

"It's guns," he said excitedly.

Two dozen Belgian-made flintlock trade guns were packed in straw. The crushing weight of other freight had broken nearly half the barrels and many of the wooden stocks. Nonetheless, they were an exceptional discovery. Painted a pale red, they profiled a brass serpent inlayed into the stock, and secured in the hammer was a piece of flint. They had been ready to load and fire for 132 years.

Information noted in *The Northwest Gun*, by Charles E. Hanson, Jr.,

Pioneers used leather cowhides for many things, including the making and repairing of shoes, boots, whips, slickers, harnesses, saddles, and bridles. **Photo by Greg Hawley**

indicates these "trade guns" represented a remarkable chapter in American history. The white man's desire for furs permitted the Indians to fulfill their desire for guns. The Indians' demands for firearms resulted in the manufacture of a sturdy and dependable flintlock. Indians could carry these lightweight weapons all day, yet the guns were powerful enough to knock down big game. Anyone could find flint to ignite the gunpowder. Because the barrels were smooth bore, not rifled, they could shoot a projectile ranging from a lead ball to a piece of river gravel without damaging the barrel. The gun became known as the Northwest Gun after its ultimate destination, the Northwest Territory. The Mackinaw Company sold them in the largest quantities. The sale price of a Northwest Gun varied due to demand. The Hudson Bay Company generally asked for 20 beaver skins per weapon.

These trade guns influenced the history of America like no other firearm. Fur trading companies relied heavily on the barter power of the Northwest Gun, and the United States government gave thousands of weapons to the Indians as partial payment for signing peace treaties. This gun was the weapon of choice for the American Indian.

The trade guns found aboard the Arabia *display a brass side plate in the shape of a sea serpent—a tradition surviving since the 1700s, when English-made Queen Anne light muskets, exhibiting a serpent, accompanied traders and explorers to America.* **Photo by Greg Hawley**

"To Be or Not..."
On the Arabia
January 2, 1989

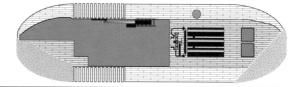

Since the beginning of the dig, we wondered if the front of the boat was intact. After washing sand off the bow for two hours we uncovered the bow's cargo hatches. We realized that our first core sample had entered the *Arabia* through the open hatch, which accounted for the lack of cargo and pine decking. It proved a lucky miss. Boxes and crates were everywhere. If the drill had pierced the boat one foot in any direction, we would have destroyed a lot of merchandise.

We were impatient to begin lifting boxes from the bow, but a lot of cargo still remained in the stern, and we needed to finish that area. Working between the paddle wheels, I uncovered a box that appeared to belong to a scholarly individual. Inside I found several books, a fancy inkwell made of amber-tinted glass, and marble bookends. The pages inside the books had turned to mush, but some of the book covers were legible: works by William Shakespeare, with a subtitle "He Is Not For A

Day, But For All Time;" "Maps of the Territories," a must for any westbound traveler; and "Poems of Ossion," something special to help pass the time on the river.

The inkwell was an exceptional device. Equipped with a rubber plunger, the user pumped air into the lower ink chamber which forced the ink to rise through a small tube leading to a funnel-shaped reservoir. After completing the writing task, the user twisted the plunger knob and let the ink flow back into the main chamber.

Other discoveries included canned peaches, lumber, harnesses, ax heads, and one dozen wood-trimmed writing slates and pre-sharpened slate pencils.

As the light faded, I discovered an additional box of boots. Three

The remains of a book by Shakespeare and a fancy, amber-tinted inkwell gave evidence of a wealthy aristocrat traveling aboard the steamer. The book's subtitle, "He is not for a day, but for all time," relates well to the Arabia.

Photo by Greg Hawley

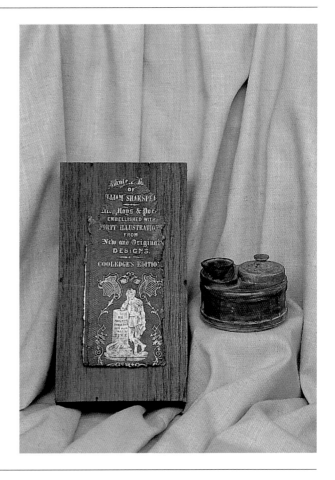

weeks ago I was jumping with joy at the sight of footwear. Now, my partners and I wondered how many lifetimes of work lay ahead preserving these leather items.

Fighting the Water
January 3, 1989

I spent the first half of the day wetting down artifacts at the lab. By noon I was back at the excavation. After successfully removing all the freight from the cargo bay on the larboard side of the *Arabia*, stretching from the stern forward to the boilers, we switched our recovery efforts to the starboard side next to the paddle wheel.

Even with nearly 16,000 gallons of water rushing to the surface each minute, and our generators and heavy equipment burning $600 of fuel per day, the water table continued to win the battle. With the starboard side of the *Arabia*'s stern and bow considerably lower—due to the arching and twisting of the hull—the aquifer defied us with four feet of unwanted water. Stubbornly we waded in with shovel, buckets, water hoses, and all our brute strength, hoping to fight our way through the muck to the cargo. We retired frustrated and exhausted. Bullheaded as we were, we could not defeat the water. We had to visit our banker and ask for more money to buy additional pumps, pipe, wire, control boxes, fuel, and another generator.

Before the excavation started, our families were certain that we could successfully dig the *Arabia* and recover the cargo for $250,000, a hefty sum for us. It was a topic I avoided with my wife. My share, amounting to $50,000, kept me awake at night, but now it seemed like chicken feed. With one more trip to the bank, our families' total investment would reach $500,000. Including the $150,000 raised from investors, we had spent $650,000 to date.

"The bank can only take our house once," I reminded my wife. "And they probably don't want any of our children."

Good Enough to Eat
January 4, 1989

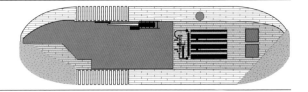

The first discovery of the day was a large crate containing dozens of boxes filled with cigars. Burnt into the top of each small box was an eagle with its wings spread and the word "Washington" arching across the top.

The defiant water table made work miserable. The sticky quagmire that entrapped boxes, crates, and barrels seemed determined to trap me as well. Stepping into the ooze, I immediately sank, my lower half slowly consumed, one inch at a time. I felt like I was living out a scene from an old Tarzan movie, where the villain steps into quicksand and slowly vanishes. I was always relieved when my feet finally touched the bottom

Jerry, left, and Greg struggled to move through the quagmire and free boxes caught in the sticky goo.   **Photo by Dave Hawley**

of the *Arabia's* wooden hull.

Tired from battling the water table, we stopped for a lunch. Compliments of Jerry, we ate cheeseburgers while discussing our next move.

"We could pot hole for the rest of the day," Jerry suggested in a hopeful tone.

"Pot hole" meant digging here and there, deviating from our plan to move progressively through the stern before starting on the bow. No one could cast any stones when it came to "pot holing." The temptation to move ahead and peek in a few boxes or barrels was a habit carried over from childhood. Who is not guilty of snooping around the house, searching out Christmas and birthday presents before the occasion?

Moving into the bow's open cargo hatch after lunch, the first box revealed more boots and shoes.

"If this footwear ever comes back in style, we're set for life," I joked.

The next box was more to my liking: three gorgeous, white stoneware pitchers manufactured by Wedgwood. With darkness closing in, we hoisted the day's final box from the cargo hold and gently set it on the main deck. When we lifted the lid, we discovered beautiful "Cathedral" bottles containing bright green pickles. Each bottle carried an oval label made of lead foil which read, "Sweet Pickles, Wells Provost & Co. 215, 217 & 219 Front St. Wholesale Depot, New York."

The pickles looked good enough to eat and Jerry proved it. Taking his knife, Jerry sliced off a small chunk of pickle and popped it in his mouth. A few chews and one swallow later, Jerry smiled and said, "They're sweet pickles, and they are great." I wanted to try one, but decided to wait a few days and see if Jerry survived.

The "Cathedral" bottle received its name for resembling stain glass windows in majestic cathedrals. Attempting to compete with English pickles, American companies used Gothic-styled bottles.

Pickled vegetables and spices were a common necessity to Americans during the 1800s since they didn't have adequate cooling for the proper long-term storage of food.

Preserving the pickles and the previously discovered bottled cherries was a challenge. The unstable nature of these items commanded the highest priority which included stabilization and regimented monitoring. To reduce the risk of bacterial growth within the bottles, we

above *Bob Hawley admires a bottle of pickles.*

right *Bright green pickles shipped in "Cathedral" bottles helped meet dietary needs of the pioneer.*
Photos by Greg Hawley

applied melted canning wax to existing corks and placed the bottles in cold storage at 36 degrees F.

That evening, I walked into my home just before midnight. The house was dark. The long days at the excavation were physically and emotionally difficult for both my wife and me. Karen, expecting our third child, felt like a widow; and my two children, Kristin and Derek, felt fatherless. Lying in bed waiting for sleep, I felt guilty. I questioned my decision to excavate this boat. It seemed selfish to risk the future of my family for the adventure. Yet the allure of buried treasure was strong, and we were so far in debt it was too late to stop. I felt addicted to the *Arabia*. With eyes heavy from work, I drifted off to sleep reliving the day's events, while dreaming of tomorrow.

Wash water was necessary to blast away thick mud that held boxes, but often it hindered salvage efforts as the excavation site filled with water.   Photo by Bob Hawley

**Old Fish
January 5, 1989**

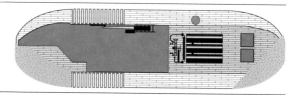

The sound of rain rushing down the gutters of my home woke me at 5:00 A.M. I ate a quick breakfast and was out the door driving toward the *Arabia*. With two miles remaining, I left the pavement behind and locked the gears of my truck into four-wheel drive. The ruts in the old road leading to the *Arabia* had deepened with our continuous use, and heavy rains transformed the entire area into a shallow lake. My truck lurched uncontrollably as I fought to keep it centered on the narrow path. Deep embankments paralleled both sides of the road. If I slowed down, I might sink in the mud and get stuck. If I sped up, I might lose control and drive over the edge. Without warning, my truck slid violently to the right and skidded over the embankment. In slow motion, the skyline tilted, and my truck crashed to a stop in the brush-entangled ditch. Luckily, my truck stayed upright and I was uninjured. On the downside, I now had a mile and a half walk through knee-deep mud to get to the *Arabia*.

Thirty minutes later, tired and very muddy, I peered down into the excavation. Mechanically speaking, the day was not going well. My truck was at the bottom of a deep ditch, and the dig site was filling with water. A generator had sprung an oil leak and shut down.

My father was working intently on repairing the generator. I pitched in to help and by lunch time, the generator was again on-line.

The day's first discovery was a box containing a variety of tinware. Later, we discovered a crate filled with sardines imported from France. The rectangular tin containers were like those found in stores today. We peeled one lid back and a foul odor smacked me in the face, and I jerked my head away trying to escape the stink. We removed the remaining tins of fish and placed them downwind of the excavation. The next and last box found on this day was full of—you guessed it—shoes. Eighty pairs to be exact.

At the end of the day there was still one item I needed to recover: my pickup truck. With tow straps and a winch, Dad, Jerry, and Dave tugged my truck free.

A Daily Ritual
January 6, 1989

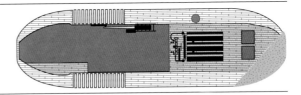

I did not drive my truck into the ditch on the way in. So far the day was starting out great.

Responsibilities at the excavation site had become a ritual. Each of us had our particular jobs. After putting on our gear, we assembled and primed our pumps for washing, rolled out hundreds of feet of four-inch hose for sand removal, and fueled and started up the earth-moving equipment. Once we turned on the hoses the physical work began.

Excavators found large quantities of food aboard the Arabia. *Although the labeling on this box reads "Fresh Cove Oysters," the smell indicated the contrary.* Photo by Greg Hawley

This decorative brass trim weighs less than two slices of bread and adorned the Arabia *with a style befitting a grand hotel.* Photo by Greg Hawley

Moving away tons of mud and lifting out thousands of pounds of artifacts each day pushed us to our limits. Occasionally, our trucks contained so many artifacts there was no more room, and we had to stop digging. Dog-tired, we returned to the lab each night to clean and inspect our discoveries. This project was thrilling beyond our imagination, but it was also life-altering.

Between the two paddle wheels, we found boxes of merchandise in staggering numbers: hundreds of pounds of hardware, tools, clothing, and food. We estimated that we had recovered 50 tons of artifacts so far.

At the end of the day, we climbed out of the cargo bay and began the final cleaning of sand off the main deck of the *Arabia's* stern. Here we discovered cast iron pots, pieces of decorative brass trim used to adorn the *Arabia*, gears for a saw mill, a forge used by the boat's blacksmith, and the *Arabia's* anchor.

Fruit Pies for the Frontier
January 7, 1989

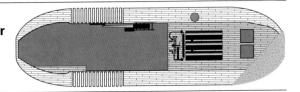

Stiff north winds and 15 degree temperatures assaulted us as we uncovered a huge box of tinware. These pristine items included seven candle molds, ten large coffee pots, four sieves, 55 cooking pans, 13 drinking cups, a set of four pails that varied in size, one pan with a lid, seven pans with handles, six bowls, three tin whale oil lamps, 12 candle holders, and three progressively-sized canisters, one inside another with hinged lids. The sale prices remained visible on the canisters: $1.00 for the smallest canister, a $1.50 for the middle size, and $2.00 for the largest; this was a seemingly huge amount of money for the 1850s.

The discoveries continued with cooking stoves, kegs of butter and pork, stacks of wooden washtubs, and boxes upon boxes of other merchandise. One box was unique. Nestled in a packing of sawdust, we found a dozen tall decorative bottles containing Western Spicemills Pepper Sauce, St. Louis.

Because of inadequate cold storage during the 1800s, the meat deteriorated quite rapidly. Early Americans used pepper sauce and other

This tinware found aboard the Arabia *was in amazing condition. So kind was the environment that prices written in ink are still legible and a century old fingerprint can still be seen.*
Photo by Greg Hawley

spices to flavor meat and cover up the rancid taste.

The labeling on the next box read, "Assorted Pie Fruit, Price and Littic, Baltimore." It astounded me to think that pioneers enjoyed a year-round variety of fruits for making pies. Opening the box was a visual treat. We found clear, tall bottles of gooseberries, blueberries, apples, rhubarb, cherries, and blackberries. The fruit's color was so deliciously bright, it inspired us to take a lunch break and admire our discovery.

Discovering this fruit again closed the distance between the past and

Pioneers used Western Spicemills Pepper Sauce to add flavor to their meals.
Photo by Greg Hawley

Pioneers dined with style on a variety of fruit pies: gooseberries, apples, blackberries, and cherries, both light and dark.   **Photo by Greg Hawley**

Superb examples of scroll flasks, like those found aboard the Arabia, *are virtually unknown.*
Photo by Greg Hawley

present. My ancestors had enjoyed more comforts than I had considered possible.

After lunch, it was back to play. The next box contained beautiful blue and green bottles packed in straw, manufactured by Christian Ihmsen and Sons, in Pittsburgh, Pennsylvania.

These decorative scroll whiskey flasks originated in the 1830s. An article from *The Mystery behind the G-IXs*, by Ralph Finch, stated that "practically every glasshouse along the river made them." They carried graceful designs in assorted colors.

Today, collectors spend thousands of dollars obtaining these once common bottles. Pristine examples, such as those found aboard the *Arabia*, are virtually unknown. Trapped in the bowels of this steamer and surrounded by mud, the glass remained pure and unblemished.

With the sun setting and north winds blowing, the temperatures dropped dangerously low. As I prepared to leave for the day, my friend

Vince Dye and his scraggy bird dog arrived to watch over the excavation. Vince normally asked about the day's discovery, but not that night.

"It's going to be a cold night. Is there enough propane in the camper to keep me from freezing to death?" Vince asked.

Eager to leave, I assured Vince he had nothing to worry about and wished him luck. By midnight, the temperatures plummeted to a -50 wind chill, causing the diesel fuel to gel in the supply lines that led to the generators. As a result, one generator shut down. Because we assembled the de-watering system in a manifold design, the pumps that remained operational were sending water backwards through the pumps that were off. To prevent water from flooding back into the site, Vince had to shut off four water valves on the inoperable wells. He completed the task, but not before spraying water drenched him to the bone.

Vince was half-frozen, exhausted, and desperate when he climbed into the sanctuary of the heated camper. With teeth chattering, he spread his sleeping bag out and stripped off his water-soaked clothing. Standing stark naked with his faithful mutt looking on, Vince realized the camper was absent of heat. The propane tank was empty—an oversight on my part. Vince frantically dressed and dashed to his truck, seeking relief from the cold. His hands shook so violently he barely got the key into the ignition, but the truck was also freezing and refused to start. Vince finally rushed back into the camper. Peeling off his clothing for the second time he climbed into his sleeping bag, but he was not alone. On the edge of the excavation and two miles from the nearest house, Vince and his flea-bitten dog snuggled together, nose to nose, skin to fur, for a very long night.

Fighting the Cold
January 8 - 10, 1989

With arctic wind chills of 40 and 50 degrees below zero cutting across the excavation site, we spent the following three days nursing generators and keeping groundwater from reclaiming the *Arabia*.

The water table continued to fight us, and with help from the bitter cold it appeared to be winning. One generator's valve froze, shutting down four de-watering pumps, while the other three starved for fuel each night from subzero temperatures. My partners and I worked around the clock protecting our investment of time, money, and dreams. Yet we could not continue this quest. If we were to gain ground and win this war against the incoming water, we needed more de-watering pumps.

Removing the Boilers
January 11, 1989

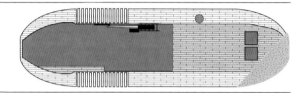

On Wednesday, the weather finally granted us relief with a projected high of 50 degrees.

While we waited for the well drillers to arrive for the installation of the additional pumps, we lifted the *Arabia*'s steam boilers and doctor from their moorings so we could reach the freight below.

We easily hoisted the steam doctor, located just behind the boilers, with the track hoe. However, removing the boilers proved more difficult. Empty, the boilers each weighed 6,000 pounds; but filled with water-soaked river sand, I estimated their individual weight at 15,000 pounds. Using both the track hoe and bulldozer, we wrestled the iron cylinders from their resting place, and laboriously dragged them up and out of the excavation site.

Installing the Final Wells
January 12 - 19, 1989

Ro-Banks prepared to pierce the earth while my partners and I assembled pipe and maneuvered it into place. We had perfected our trade considerably since breaking ground months earlier. Over the next two days we lowered four more well casings into place.

After installing the twentieth well casing, we began the laborious job of lowering pumps and motors into place, wiring pumps to generators, and welding together hundreds of feet of discharge pipe. For the next seven days we worked diligently to complete the de-watering system, while nurturing tons of artifacts previously recovered.

**Medicine for the Frontier
January 20, 1989**

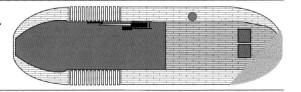

We now had 20 wells with a pumping capacity of 20,000 gallons of water per minute. Within a few hours the water table dropped below the *Arabia* to a depth of 45 feet. Watching the water retreat downward into the sand gave us a sense of victory. Persistence, modern technology, and a bit of good luck created our success.

We turned on the wash hoses, and a host of barrels, boxes, and small kegs appeared. The first box contained 12 bottles of castor oil.

"This reminds me of the good old days. You should try some, you'll love the taste," my dad said. Dad's encouragement did not impress or persuade me.

Next, we found another box containing a variety of medicines. Many of the medicines were in unlabeled bottles, while others included Nerve and Bone Liniment, McGuire Druggist, St. Louis, Mo.; Mexican Mustang, Dr. D. Jones Expectorant; and small round pills of an unknown substance.

Beside the medicine we found a box containing American Vermilion, which was probably used for trade with the Indians. Indians mixed vermilion with the sticky juice of the prickly pear or mucilage obtained from boiling beaver tails. Indians rubbed the mixture on leather or their skin for decoration and ceremonial purposes.

By the 1850s, the Indians were nearly as diverse in their needs and wants as the white man. According to historians Arthur Woodward and Charles Hanson, Jr., settlers and Indians both shared a common need for many items found on the *Arabia*, but they often used them in different ways. Indians often used sewing thimbles to adorn pouches and clothing. By punching a small hole through the apex of the cone, Indians could attach them to leather fringe by passing the end through the opening and tying a knot. Thimbles clustered together became known as "tinklers" for the sound they made. Thimbles replaced the more traditional ornament made from the points of hollowed-out deer hooves.

Indians did not limit the use of thimbles to "tinklers." They occasionally flattened out the thimbles and formed them into razor sharp points used on arrows for hunting and war.

The final crates removed from the *Arabia*'s stern contained an overwhelming cargo of food, eating utensils, hardware, cloth, and tools. This marked the halfway point in salvaging the steamer. Recovering cargo from the forward section should progress quickly now that we had conquered the water table. I knew my wife and children would be thrilled with the news, but I also dreaded the day this adventure would end.

Medicine destined for the frontier included castor oil, liniments, expectorants, and unidentified small round pills.
Photo by Greg Hawley

Half the Cargo
is Out

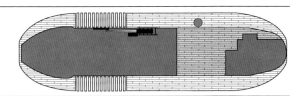

Frozen Charlotte
January 21, 1989

A s I adorned myself with my traditional digging apparel of rubber waders, coat, gloves, and hat, others pulled up deck planking from the *Arabia*'s bow. The first box that caught my eye was two feet long and approximately eleven inches square. I grabbed the box on either end and pulled upwards, but the box barely moved. Dad noticed I was struggling and offered to help.

"I could use the help," I told Dad. "But the contents in this box are all mine. It's so heavy it must be filled with gold bars."

Dad was instantly beside me, and together we lifted the box from the cargo hold. Instead of gold, the box had lead printers type inside.

The writing on the box of printers type read: "Thompson and Butts, Council Bluffs, Iowa." Although little is known about Mr. Butts, the accomplishments of Charles Blancher Thompson were many.

According to the *Annals of Iowa*, on February 10, 1835, Charles Blancher Thompson, at the age of 21, became a member of the Church of Jesus Christ of Latter Day Saints. He was confirmed by Joseph Smith, founder of the church, and later ordained by Joseph Smith and Sidney Rigdon. Thompson spent much of his young life working for the Mormon church. In January 1851, Thompson began publishing a small monthly magazine entitled *Zion's Harbinger and Baneemy's Organ*, in which he proclaimed himself as the Chief Teacher and spiritual leader. On September 9, 1853, along with a new printing press, Thompson traveled to Council Bluffs and established a community named "Preparation." Thompson attracted followers to his spiritual community, and with strict rules enforced through claims of prophetic authority, successfully maintained the settlement for many years.

The next box instantly drew everyone's attention. Its construction indicated that a craftsman had made this box by fitting together multiple pieces of wood in a precise arrangement. The joints were so tight that only a small amount of mud had penetrated the box. The box held a draw knife, a miter box, saws, mallets, scribes, chisels, screwdrivers, and files, wrenches, vises, augers, wood planes of all sizes, and one knife marked with the trademark "Green River."

The "Green River" knives were popular with fur traders of the far West. Produced by the John Russell Company, in Greenfield, Massachusetts, the firm stamped the "Green River" name on the blade near the knife handle. It inspired the phrase, "If you must stab a man, make sure it is clear to 'Green River.'"

One hour after Dad began removing items from this box, it appeared empty. As Dad scooped out the remaining mud, he discovered a black wool stocking stuffed in one corner. He unrolled the sock to find a child-like figure made of porcelain. Only two and one-half inches tall, she was pure white with black eyes and only a bonnet painted upon her head—a remarkable treasure. Perhaps the doll was a keepsake, a traveling companion for the long trip west, or a cherished memento from a loved one left far behind.

Since that savored moment of my father's discovery, we have learned a great deal about this exquisite doll.

Authors George Eleanor, in *The Dolls of Yesterday*, and Patricia R. Smith, in *Antique Collector's Dolls*, have contributed to the written history of this doll. Many believe the story surrounding this tiny figure to be true. In 1833, a young woman, Charlotte, left her home to go to a New Year's Eve Ball with her suitor, Charles. As she settled into his open sleigh for the 15-mile journey, her mother handed her a woolen blanket for warmth. Charlotte refused the blanket, saying it would wrinkle her silken gown.

Charlotte and Charles were soon gliding across the snow as starlight flashed above through the forest canopy. With numb hands, Charles fought to maintain the reins, and Charlotte spoke briefly of being exceedingly cold. As the miles passed, ice formed on Charles' brow, while Charlotte, with a weak voice, exclaimed, "I'm growing warmer now." The horses continued until the lights of the ballroom at last came into view. The sleigh had barely halted when Charles stepped down and turned to reach for the hand of his beloved. Like a statue, Charlotte remained motionless. Charles took her hand—it was as cold as the night. Charles carried Charlotte's lifeless body into the ballroom. Kneeling beside her, he cried mournfully and later died of a broken heart.

William Lorenzo Carter immortalized this tale through his ballad "Fair Charlotte," which was popular throughout the United States. Moms and dads sang it to their children at bedtime, reminding them, "If you'll just wear your coat and listen to your parents, you won't end up like Fair Charlotte."

By 1850, craftsman began producing a variety of small dolls known to collectors as "Frozen Charlottes."

Discovered in a box filled with carpentry tools, this Frozen Charlotte doll escaped damage tucked inside a black wool stocking. **Photo by Greg Hawley**

A Big Problem
January 22, 1989

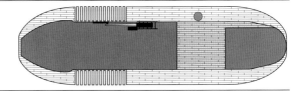

The next morning my father, brother, and I huddled together to discuss a serious problem.

"The excavation discharge water has eroded the river bank where it enters the river," Dad explained. "The water coming from our de-watering system is cutting a huge gully, devouring land and trees, while slowly eating its way back from the river."

I drove to the river's edge where our discharge water once flowed over the bank and into the Missouri River. To my horror, the river bank was gone. The discharge water had cut a giant swath of earth, creating a canyon 200 yards long, 25 feet deep, and 30 feet across.

The size of the hole and the rate at which it was increasing represented a big threat to the excavation and the Sortor's farmland. We were just days from completing the dig, but if the erosion broke through the trees and reached the unprotected farm, tons of top soil each day would erode into the river. Short of shutting down the excavation, we could not stop the erosion. We returned to work, just hoping the remaining barrier of trees and underbrush would hold back the water for a few more days.

The first box we uncovered that day contained two-man saws. I admired yet pitied the men who once used them. The business of felling and sawing trees was meant for men with brute strength and stamina. A day behind one of these saws would greatly enhance anyone's appreciation for modern technology.

Our next discovery was another box containing two dozen trade guns manufactured in Belgium. As with those previously discovered, the weight of other freight had broken most of the stocks and snapped several barrels.

These guns were in the deepest and most inaccessible part of the cargo hold. On an earlier journey, abolitionists tried to smuggle weapons to Kansas aboard the *Arabia*, but Missourians confiscated the guns at Lexington. Fearing Missourian pro-slavers might come aboard

With discharge water threatening to erode the Sortor's farm, Florence and Bob Hawley work hard to remove sand from the Arabia*'s bow.*   **Photo by Sonie Lieber**

A merchant on the frontier ordered these items for his store. Found in a single oak barrel they represent the needs of his customers.   **Photo by Greg Hawley**

The Sharps carbine shown here bears the serial number 17739, authenticating this carbine as one of the original weapons seized at Lexington, Missouri, by pro-slavers on March 13, 1856. For soldiers and hunters the dependable Sharps became known as "Old Reliable." Native Americans called the Sharps "shoot today, kill tomorrow," for its long range capability.

Rifle courtesy of Don Hildebrand

Photo by Greg Hawley

the *Arabia* again, perhaps the crew hid the guns in an area that was difficult to reach.

We then uncovered dozens of kegs, boxes, and one large oak barrel lying on its side. It took five of us two hours to unload the 350 pounds of tools and hardware from the barrel.

The day ended with so many artifacts that I had to stack them on the floor and pile them on the front seat of my truck. I barely had room to steer.

Tasting the Past
January 23, 1989

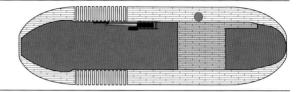

We unearthed new discoveries quickly: a box of wool felt hats, door knobs and related hardware, coffee grinders, cases of cognac, hatchets, nutmeg, kegs of black pine tar, six kegs of square nails weighing 100 pounds each, and numerous other items.

Suddenly, the roar of an airplane interrupted our work. I looked up and saw a red plane swooping down. The plane circled and buzzed the excavation for over an hour.

The airplane finally left, and the day slipped into night. I had already recovered three cases of cognac when a fourth crate came into view. I lifted the lid and saw the bottoms of 12 bottles. I slipped off my clumsy rubber gloves and pushed aside the sawdust packing. Using my right hand, I gripped one bottle firmly and lifted it free. Just as the bottle cleared the box, the cork dropped out. The bottle began pouring its precious liquid upon the muddy floor. Panicked, I quickly turned the bottle upright, trying to save the contents. To my surprise, the bottle contained champagne. Flipping the bottle had caused the fluid to spew violently in all directions, striking me squarely in the face. Briefly paralyzed by the unexpected explosion, I struggled to spit out this foreign concoction. Jerry stood calmly before me, grinning as wide as the Missouri.

"Well don't just stand there and drip; how is it?"

Dripping from elbows, chin, nose, ears, and hair, I looked about and noticed that everyone was scrambling toward me.

"How was it?" my Dad asked. I concentrated on the remaining taste still lingering in my mouth and then cautiously licked my lips for confirmation. "Actually, it's great."

I passed the bottle to Jerry who took a drink that would make any sailor proud. Gathering together, we each drank from the old bottle. We enjoyed it, not for the liquor, but for the camaraderie it sparked. Time stood still as we found ourselves absorbed with the joy of discovery and the value of good friends and close family. Forty-five feet below ground

Jerry and his partners savored a taste of champagne. Experts have disputed the claim that champagne could still fizz after 132 years, but salvagers of the Arabia *know differently.*
Photo by Dave Hawley

level, standing on the main deck of the *Arabia*, only the surrounding darkness heard our merriment and laughter.

I had just arrived at home when the phone rang. It was my father. "The newspapers and TV stations are calling, and they want to visit the dig," Dad said.

"I'll bet the pilot in the red airplane tipped them off," I replied.

More rare than buried treasure are the times that the government does not try to dip its hands into someone else's discovery. Fearing state officials may try to declare the *Arabia* a historical site and shut down the excavation, we had told only close friends and relatives about the dig. There is an old adage I will never forget. "When it comes to the government, it is often easier to ask for forgiveness than to get permission."

Watch Out for the Water
January 24, 1989

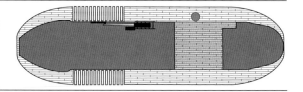

Our work had barely begun when we discovered the tree that sank the *Arabia*. Protruding through the *Arabia*'s larboard side and 12 feet back from the bow, the tree stabbed deep into the cargo bay. Smashing and ripping both the boat and cargo, the blunt end of the snag pierced a full ten feet into the steamer. After tearing through three inches of oak hull, the tree destroyed a huge amount of freight, including three cases of champagne and half a crate of precious blue and green scroll bottles.

The stern of the *Arabia* held vast amounts of treasure, but the bow held even more. We could barely find a place to stand without stepping on boxes of cargo. In all directions we found hundreds of crates of westbound necessities.

Candles were among the most interesting discoveries of the day. Inside, the candles were in nearly perfect shape, except for the wicks. Cotton wicks dissolved one inch into the candles on both ends. The candles consisted of tallow (animal fat), not wax, and ridges running down the candles confirmed the manufacturer had pressed them into shape.

The items we removed included the broken crates and shattered bottles from around the snag. In the foremost portion of the *Arabia*'s bow, the mud remained knee-deep, and our movements slowed to an agonizing pace. We routinely needed help to free ourselves from the sticky gumbo. Having worked in these muddy conditions for several weeks, we grew accustomed to the work environment and we seldom complained—until that day.

Unknown to us, the *Arabia*'s hull was acting like a circular dam, preventing groundwater from pouring in at the lowest point of the excavation. As a result, the oak hull was holding back an immense amount of water pressure. That is, until we removed the freight that lay on and around the snag. Without warning, a tidal wave of water exploded through the hole and began filling the excavation. Mired in mud above our knees, we fought to escape, but the water rose with

Improved Press'd Candles, manufactured by Jacob Keller of Louisville, Kentucky, illuminated homes and businesses on the frontier. Manufacturers made these candles from tallow, not wax.
Photo by Greg Hawley

frightening speed. Dad was in the lowest spot, and within five seconds the water was above his waist and still climbing. Never had I experienced anything so frightful. "Get out," I yelled, while struggling to save myself. The water level continued to climb and I feared a tragedy was at hand, but abruptly the onslaught stopped. The sand surrounding the snag had miraculously resealed the hole in the *Arabia*'s hull. As we helped each other free, all of us looked a bit pale.

"A short man would have died down there," I joked later.

My partners and I now used extreme caution when working in the area around the snag. Water pressure climbed to its bursting point, then surged into the *Arabia* several times daily. Since our brush with death, we stood on boards and no longer let our feet sink deep in the mud.

Arriving at home just ahead of midnight, I had to tell Karen the story of the water rushing in. Half drowsy, Karen seemed unimpressed with our narrow escape.

"Yes, dear, whatever you say, dear," she muttered.

"I guess you had to be there," I thought to myself. My eyes closed for only a moment when Karen woke me by tugging on my foot and yelling. "Get down from there, Greg! You're going to kill yourself and me too." I had somehow climbed to the top of our bed's headboard, and, according to Karen, was yelling, "Get out, get out, the water is coming in!"

The Word is Out

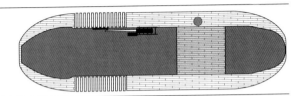

A Voice of Concern
January 25, 1989

"Y ou're not going to like what the paper has to say," I told Karen as I showed her the headline.

"'GOD SAVE THE *ARABIA*,'" she read. "I can't believe the newspaper would write something so critical about us. How can they be so certain we will fail?"

Since the pilot had tipped off the news agencies, we granted several interviews and opened the excavation to the media. We had grown accustomed to fighting water, mud, and the elements of winter; but dealing with media controversy was a new challenge.

News of the excavation angered many local historians. However, it was not the dig that incensed them, it was who was doing the digging.

"Those artifacts should be boxed up and shipped to the Smithsonian," said one historian.

"Those people are not qualified, the collection will be ruined," said another.

When I arrived at the excavation, officials from Missouri and Kansas pulled in behind me. Because of the newspaper and TV coverage, I knew they would eventually show up to inspect the operation. Their presence made me a bit apprehensive, but after speaking with our archeologist they seemed satisfied with our efforts.

After our "guests" departed, we resumed work. As I lifted a box, I contemplated the enormous task that lay ahead. The estimated weight of the collection was over 150 tons and still growing. By law, the artifacts were ours to sell, but who would buy a pair of wet boots or a muddy water-soaked hat? We would have to preserve them to sell them, and preservation could take years, perhaps decades.

As I put the last load of artifacts in my truck, the news headline crept back into my thoughts. For a moment, I wondered if the academic community was right. Maybe families like ours should leave the excavating to the professionals. Looking at my truck heaping with artifacts, and thinking of the many tons piling up at the lab, for the first time I questioned our chances of success. Then I remembered what my dad often says: "Persistence and determination alone are omnipotent."

Finger Prints
January 26, 1989

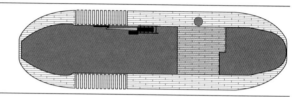

Once again, I awoke with heavy rains beating the side of my home. Despite the bone-chilling weather, the work continued. Our fuel bill now exceeded $650 a day just to keep the hole free of water. The overall cost of excavating the *Arabia* was approaching $700,000. If we had known the expense necessary to excavate the *Arabia*'s treasures, I doubt we would ever have started. The mental pressure of owing hundreds of thousands of dollars to the bank made things tense at home. My wife and I could lose everything if we failed: our home, cars, business, and our pride.

Fortunately, our salvaging was almost complete. Soon we would silence the generators, and the water would again consume the *Arabia*. It was a sobering thought. The *Arabia* had provided high adventure in a way we had never experienced nor imagined. When the time came to throw the switch and watch the groundwater rush in and recapture her, I knew life would become instantly boring. I thought of slowing down to enjoy the last few days, but the cost of keeping the hole open gave me a guilty conscience.

Despite sulky attitudes, my partners and I continued our search and discovered a hand truck and cargo hooks in the forward hold.

The hand truck had a heavy oak frame with two handles on one end and supported two large iron wheels on the other. Judging from its size and weight, no man short on strength ever used it to tote cargo aboard the *Arabia*.

The discovery of cargo hooks also provided new insights into the cargo loading and distribution techniques used by the *Arabia*'s crew. Unevenly distributed weight made steering difficult and navigation of shallow water hazardous. Each time the steamer stopped to load or unload, the crew redistributed the cargo. Workers on the boat used the cargo hooks to pull freight through the cargo hull. Builders of the *Arabia* installed wooden planks butted end to end on both the starboard and larboard side of the steamer and running parallel to the keel, from bow to stern. Bridging the ribs of the *Arabia*'s hull, these crawl ways made the movement of freight and the leveling of the boat a task of pulling and sliding.

We also found boxes of weight scales. The most interesting scale was a platform scale displaying the names Fairbanks and Livingston Roggen. Today, scales throughout the world continue to boast the name Fairbanks.

The companies of Fairbanks and Livingston Roggen helped manufacture this platform scale. Scales throughout the world continue to boast the name Fairbanks. **Photo by Greg Hawley**

Back at the lab, we cleaned and stabilized the day's bounty. I chose as my first task a box of looking glasses. A thin layer of mud covered the glass on the top mirror. I wondered who was the last person to have their image reflected in this mirror. Like trying to catch a ghost, I impulsively wiped a swath of mud from the reflective surface and quickly looked. The image staring back was my own. I felt silly and turned the mirror over to clean the back. I had barely begun when something caught my eye: a set of fingerprints. In the mirror's reflective backing was a nearly perfect set of prints. The worker who applied the coating must have handled the mirror before the solution dried. A moment earlier, I felt foolish trying to use a mirror to see into the past. My error was not that I looked at the mirror; it was that I used the wrong side.

Framed in wood, most of the mirror's reflective surface remained intact, despite its long submersion in water. Pressed into the reflective surface on the back are the fingerprints of the maker.
Photos by Greg Hawley

**Don't Let the
Bed Bugs Bite
January 27, 1989**

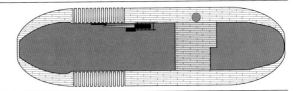

As I did everyday, I paused on the edge of the excavation and admired both the *Arabia* and the huge hole we had dug. I was extremely proud of what my partners, family, friends, and I had done.

Within the hour, my partners arrived and we were back at work washing a layer of century-old mud off the steamer. With several boxes revealed, we quieted the hoses and inspected the contents. One large box held hundreds of nearly-perfect rubber shoes.

The rubber shoes found aboard the *Arabia* were manufactured by Ford Rubber Co., N. Brunswick, N.J., Coodys Pat. 1849, and Goodyears Shoe Co., Naugatuck, Ct., Patent 1844. To prevent deterioration, we froze all rubber artifacts in blocks of ice.

Ford Rubber Co. and Goodyears Shoe Co. manufactured the 250 rubber shoes discovered aboard the Arabia. *These rubber shoes are the only ones known to exist from the mid-1850s.*
Photos by Greg Hawley

Next, we discovered a large number of bed keys. Americans used them to assemble the type of beds which used ropes to support the mattresses. As with most artifacts, the value of an item depends greatly on its story. From "Straining Up a Cord Bed" I have learned that before the invention of box springs or water beds, our ancestors rested on mattresses stuffed with horse hair, straw, or corn husks. Hemp ropes crisscrossed through a wood frame and supported the mattress. Unfortunately, the ropes stretched with frequent use. To insure a comfortable slumber, the ropes required frequent tightening. The mattresses were notorious for becoming infested with bugs. At night, these tiny creatures crawled from their hiding places to bite anyone who rested upon their home. The combination of these two unfortunate conditions resulted in the bedtime saying, "Sleep tight, don't let the bed bugs bite. But if they do, take your shoe and break their little heads in two." Stinging bug bites combined with sagging mattresses eventually made rope beds obsolete. However, rope beds had one attribute that modern beds don't; our ancestors could discourage unwanted guests with a bed wrench in hand and hemp ropes to loosen.

With the trucks fully loaded by 6:00 P.M., it was time to start the second shift. We cleaned newly discovered artifacts and inspected thousands of previously recovered treasures for any signs of deterioration. Leaning over sinks and washing artifacts four and five hours each night after a long day of digging was back-breaking work. Every few minutes I heard a groan, and someone arched their back and rolled their neck and shoulders, seeking relief. When we used the last of our strength, we retreated to our homes. For me, even a rope bed with bed bugs would not have prevented a deep slumber.

Boot Pistols
January 28, 1989

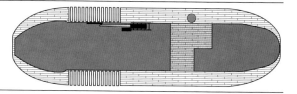

Traveling to the dig in a pouring rain, I found myself wondering what day of the week it was.

We were in the final stretch of the excavation, with the cargo in the

Greg Hawley carefully holds a single-barrel shotgun.   Photo by Dave Hawley

Firearms and related supplies recovered from the Arabia *include pistols, rifles, shotguns, bullet molds, ramrods, nipples, percussion caps, lead shot, and brass powder flasks.* Photo by Greg Hawley

bow of the *Arabia* completely removed. Only the cargo beneath where the boilers rested remained untouched. While Dave and Jerry were removing freight from the larboard side, my father and I uncovered two boxes on the starboard. One contained 14 boot pistols. Equipped with walnut hand grips, the pistols were .31 caliber single shot, single action, percussion cap weapons. Commonly known as pocket or belt-size pistols, their condition was so pristine they looked ready to fire. The second box contained two double-barrel shotguns, Belgian made; three single-barrel shotguns; and one rifle with no visible markings.

Loading the day's discovery into our trucks for the trip home, my father said teasingly, "No boots and shoes? We can't go home without some boots and shoes."

He was right. For the first time in many days, we had found no footwear.

A Change
of Direction

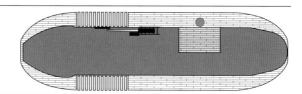

The excavation was nearing its end. The first time I mentioned digging up a boat to Karen, she was in the hospital having just given birth to our second child, Kristin.

"We're going to be rich and have a big house on the hill," I had told her.

Karen gave me a glance that said, "I've heard that story before."

I could not blame her pessimism. I was always coming up with a rags to riches scheme that never quite made it past the rags. In the hospital, Karen's interest was only with the treasure wearing a pink bow and sleeping quietly in her arms.

Three years later I was digging treasure, but my prediction of becoming monetarily rich was not coming true. The *Arabia*'s treasure was valuable well beyond the cost of the excavation, but we could not sell it. During a partner's meeting the previous evening, we unanimously decided the most priceless thing discovered aboard the *Arabia* was not the cargo, but the story it told. Each time we opened a new box of merchandise, we understood more fully the needs and wants of the westward traveler. Each time we looked in a box containing personal belongings, we immersed ourselves in the life of that individual. Whether the items represented a poor traveler or a rich one, we instantly knew what that person held most precious in their life. Inside their boxes were the things chosen above all else in the world to move west.

The *Arabia* had changed us. Once a small band of treasure hunters looking for all that glittered, we had moved beyond that narrowly focused mentality. We were now fledgling historians resolving not to sell the *Arabia* or her cargo.

The decision to save the *Arabia*'s treasure was a difficult one. We realized the need to preserve the cargo would be expensive and life-consuming. Unless we ultimately displayed the treasure, all our previous efforts would be for nothing. From this time forward we had a new dream: create a museum to host the *Arabia*'s artifacts and share the story with the world.

Mark Twain was correct in *Following the Equator* when he wrote: "To get the full value of joy, you must have someone to divide it with."

My wife and I would have to wait for another opportunity to have a big house on the hill.

At the excavation I sensed a new vigor among my partners. Having

Collectors have documented over 300 unique patterns on these beautiful buttons. Excavators discovered 109 patterns aboard the Arabia.
Photo by Greg Hawley

decided to create a museum and share our discovery increased our motivation. This was our chance to contribute to society and leave something behind besides a tombstone.

Our earlier discoveries seemed minuscule compared to the shoes and boots found beneath where the boilers sat. By day's end, we had four pickup trucks nearly full of muddy footwear.

Despite the quantities of boots and shoes, we found a host of other treasures. Buttons were the most numerous and beautiful discovery. We had found them made of rubber, brass, horn, wood, and china. China buttons numbered in the thousands and were pure white or had a calico pattern. Makers of calico buttons mass-produced them with button-making machines invented in 1840. The colorful patterns on the calico buttons matched the popular calico fabrics of the time. So favored were these buttons that collectors have charted over 300 patterns.

No Time to Waste
January 30, 1989

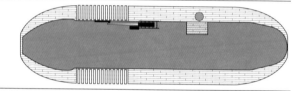

I took my daily trip down to the river's edge to inspect the ever-widening canyon created by our discharge water. This man-made river gave me sleepless nights. I wondered when it would break free of the trees and attack the Sortor's farm. Each day, the distance I walked toward it was smaller. Today, my trek went no farther than the edge of the field. I peered over the embankment and saw only one tree and its roots standing in the way of disastrous erosion.

Back at the excavation, we quickened the pace. We established two work parties: one to complete the recovery of the remaining artifacts, the other to remove key components of the *Arabia*.

We had to keep wooden items wet to prevent deterioration, but could not afford to build a swimming pool 171 feet in length and 54 feet in width to hold the entire steamer. Plus the cost of preserving such an enormous structure would be millions of dollars. We selected only two large wooden pieces of the *Arabia* for future display in the museum: the stern and the superstructure that supported the larboard engine and

Excavators discovered a variety of whale oil lamps including these fancy glass lamps featuring a double-wick design for better lighting. **Photo by Greg Hawley**

paddle wheel. We sadly left the remaining portion of the *Arabia*'s empty hull behind.

My father and brother removed the larboard engine, paddle wheel, and supporting superstructure. Using wash hoses, they removed sand throughout the day and into the evening. It was a difficult and dangerous process. The 28-foot wheel was tilting dangerously to the starboard side, and removing too much sand might have caused the structure to collapse.

Meanwhile, Jerry and I recovered more artifacts, including a box of glass whale oil lamps.

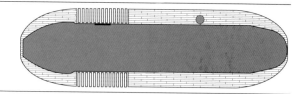

Lifting Out the Engine
January 31, 1989

Today we started earlier than usual for two big reasons: the threat of eroding the field and an up-coming cold front. Weather reports projected the temperature at 12 degrees below zero—an 84 degree change in 24 hours.

We spent the day, sadly, removing the final boxes of treasure from the *Arabia*: rubber shoes manufactured by Goodyears, knives, forks, spoons, and clothing.

The clothing found aboard the *Arabia* was far more valuable than any fancy ballroom gown or gentleman's suit from the same time period. It represented those pioneers who worked hard clearing the land and building their homes. Average people made this country great, and the clothing found on the *Arabia* was a looking glass into their personal lives.

The day ended with the raising of the larboard steam engine. Dangling from the crane's boom cable, the engine swung back and forth with a slow rhythm, as if waving good-bye to the *Arabia* below.

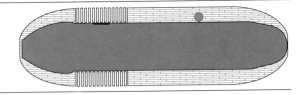

One Cent
February 1-8, 1989

The north winds were howling and the weatherman was right, the temperature was 12 degrees below zero. The day began by washing away sand from where the larboard engine had rested. It was imperative that these large structures were as light as possible before we tried to hoist them free.

The washing was underway when a friend who was helping called out, "Hey, did someone drop this penny?" He threw the coin to Dad, who was standing in water a considerable distance away. With an instinctive left-handed grab, Dad reached out with a gloved hand caked in mud and snagged the coin. Early on, we had learned to laugh off coins we discovered. Dad and Jerry were both guilty of "salting" down the excavation with money brought from home. Slipping coins into a box or crate and then covering it back up with mud, they patiently waited for someone else to discover the contents. More than once, someone cried out with joy upon discovering a handful of coins, only to find the dates were post-1856. Jerry and Dad then laughed themselves

The last artifact found at the excavation was an 1856 cent piece. Considering its date, excavators agreed it was an appropriate way to end the "thrill of discovery."
Photo by Greg Hawley

silly. This time the joke was on Dad—the copper cent piece was dated 1856, the year the *Arabia* sank, and it was in mint condition!

The total sum of money found aboard the *Arabia* now stood at 26 cents. Not only was this coin a fitting finale to the treasures discovered aboard the *Arabia*, but it also provided an opportunity to see a great one-handed catch.

For the next ten days, we focused our work on the removal of the stern, larboard paddle wheel, and the huge timbers that supported it. For eight of those days the temperature stalled near zero and the wind chill dipped to 30 degrees below. Physically, these were some of the most painful days since the excavation began.

The Last Piece
February 9, 1989

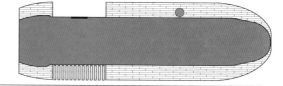

On February 9, we lifted the stern free, marking the last piece removed from the *Arabia*. We estimated the total weight of artifacts at 200 tons, the world's largest collection of pre-Civil War artifacts ever discovered.

As predicted, life suddenly seemed boring. Everyday for months, I had felt adrenaline flowing through my veins. But those moments of anticipating the contents of an unopened box were over.

Two days later and with only one foot of earth remaining before erosion cut into the Sortor's farm, we shut down the de-watering pumps. The excavation became eerily quiet. For nearly three months the rumble of diesel generators had filled the air. Now only the wind whistled around us. As the darkness dropped, the water rose, slowly entombing the *Arabia*. It was an emotional moment, like saying farewell to a good friend. We felt privileged and honored to have experienced such an adventure. Yet at that moment, no one was smiling in our group. Silently, the towering walls of sand that surrounded the *Arabia* began to bleed with water as the hole filled. One timber at a time, the *Arabia* was drowning for the second and last time. Physically and financially exhausted, our families stood in silence as the water

The stern section was the last piece removed from the Arabia.
Photo by Dave Hawley

recaptured the Great White *Arabia*.

Excavating the *Arabia* was like shaking hands with the pioneers. I had gone beyond the mere written words of history. I had met my forefathers through the items most precious in their lives. I had seen them through their innovative technology and fine craftsmanship. I had looked upon them in color through their fashionable clothing and decorative fabrics. I had filled my lungs with their aromas of tobacco, spices, and perfume, and tasted their champagne. I had held in my arms the bones of a drowned mule and bones of a meal never eaten. By excavating the steamboat *Arabia* and its westbound cargo, I had come to know and understand my ancestors for the first time.

When excavators turned off the de-watering pumps, water reclaimed the Arabia. For the next three weeks, workers refilled the hole with 200,000 cubic yards of sand.
Photo by Dave Hawley

The Arabia: Cargo Distribution

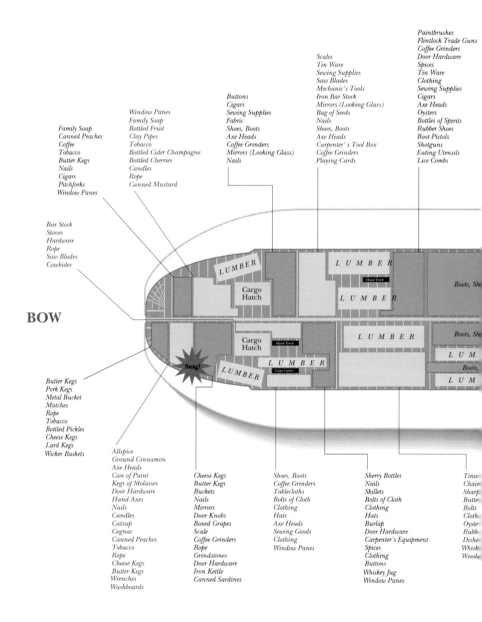

Paintbrushes
Flintlock Trade Guns
Coffee Grinders
Door Hardware
Spices
Tin Ware
Clothing
Sewing Supplies
Cigars
Axe Heads
Oysters
Bottles of Spirits
Rubber Shoes
Boot Pistols
Shotguns
Eating Utensils
Lice Combs

Scales
Tin Ware
Sewing Supplies
Saw Blades
Mechanic's Tools
Iron Bar Stock
Mirrors (Looking Glass)
Bag of Seeds
Nails
Shoes, Boots
Axe Heads
Carpenter's Tool Box
Coffee Grinders
Playing Cards

Buttons
Cigars
Sewing Supplies
Fabric
Shoes, Boots
Axe Heads
Coffee Grinders
Mirrors (Looking Glass)
Nails

Window Panes
Family Soap
Bottled Fruit
Clay Pipes
Tobacco
Bottled Cider Champagne
Bottled Cherries
Candles
Rope
Canned Mustard

Family Soap
Canned Peaches
Coffee
Tobacco
Butter Kegs
Nails
Cigars
Pitchforks
Window Panes

Bar Stock
Stoves
Hardware
Rope
Saw Blades
Cowhides

BOW

LUMBER
LUMBER
Hand Truck
Boots, Sh

Cargo Hatch
LUMBER

Cargo Hatch
Hand Truck
LUMBER
Boots, Sh

Snag!
LUMBER
Cargo Carrier
LUM

LUMBER
Boots,

LUM

Butter Kegs
Pork Kegs
Metal Bucket
Matches
Rope
Tobacco
Bottled Pickles
Cheese Kegs
Lard Kegs
Wicker Baskets

Allspice
Ground Cinnamon
Axe Heads
Can of Paint
Kegs of Molasses
Door Hardware
Hand Axes
Nails
Candles
Catsup
Cognac
Canned Peaches
Tobacco
Rope
Cheese Kegs
Butter Kegs
Wrenches
Washboards

Cheese Kegs
Butter Kegs
Buckets
Nails
Mirrors
Door Knobs
Boxed Grapes
Scale
Coffee Grinders
Rope
Grindstones
Door Hardware
Iron Kettle
Canned Sardines

Shoes, Boots
Coffee Grinders
Tablecloths
Bolts of Cloth
Clothing
Hats
Axe Heads
Sewing Goods
Clothing
Window Panes

Sherry Bottles
Nails
Skillets
Bolts of Cloth
Clothing
Hats
Burlap
Door Hardware
Carpenter's Equipment
Spices
Clothing
Buttons
Whiskey Jug
Window Panes

Tinw
Chair
Sharp
Butte
Bolts
Cloth
Oyste
Rubb
Dishe
Whisk
Woode

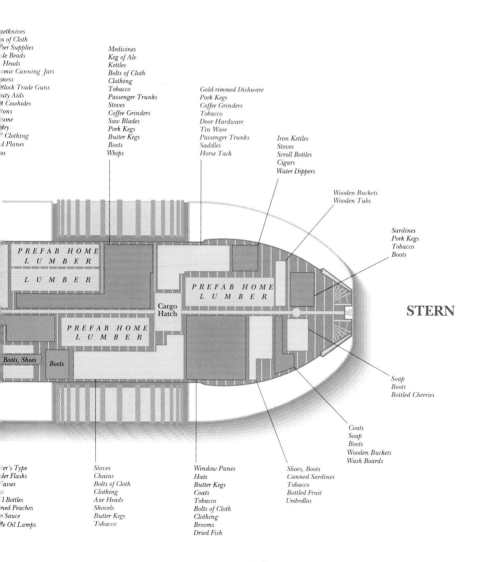

etknives
s of Cloth
her Supplies
le Beads
Heads
mic Canning Jars
ness
tlock Trade Guns
uty Aids
t Cowhides
ons
ume
dry
Clothing
l Planes
us

Medicines
Keg of Ale
Kettles
Bolts of Cloth
Clothing
Tobacco
Passenger Trunks
Stoves
Coffee Grinders
Saw Blades
Pork Kegs
Butter Kegs
Boots
Whips

Gold-rimmed Dishware
Pork Kegs
Coffee Grinders
Tobacco
Door Hardware
Tin Ware
Passenger Trunks
Saddles
Horse Tack

Iron Kettles
Stoves
Scroll Bottles
Cigars
Water Dippers

Wooden Buckets
Wooden Tubs

Sardines
Pork Kegs
Tobacco
Boots

PREFAB HOME
LUMBER

LUMBER

PREFAB HOME
LUMBER

Cargo
Hatch

STERN

PREFAB HOME
LUMBER

Boots, Shoes   *Boots*

Soap
Boots
Bottled Cherries

Coats
Soap
Boots
Wooden Buckets
Wash Boards

er's Type
der Flasks
asses
l Bottles
ned Peaches
Sauce
e Oil Lamps

Stoves
Chains
Bolts of Cloth
Clothing
Axe Heads
Shovels
Butter Kegs
Tobacco

Window Panes
Hats
Butter Kegs
Coats
Tobacco
Bolts of Cloth
Clothing
Brooms
Dried Fish

Shoes, Boots
Canned Sardines
Tobacco
Bottled Fruit
Umbrellas

⊢ 10 feet ⊣

CHAPTER 11

Norman

Norman Sortor's grandfather, Elisha Sortor, and his wife, Effie Ann, came from Allegany County, New York, in 1857, and settled in the town of Quindaro, Kansas, just one mile south and slightly east of where the *Arabia* sank in 1856. Seven years later, on November 17, 1864, Elisha purchased 36 acres for the sum of seven dollars per acre from Mary Coon, a Wyandotte Indian.

The land bordered the Missouri River on the Kansas side. As the years passed, the river moved north and east, and eventually Elisha's 36-acre investment grew to 100 acres; the farmer's land on the Missouri side shrank by an equal amount.

Elisha and Effie Ann had three sons and a daughter: Henry, Charles, Cynthia, and Norman's father, Fred. The family divided the ownership of the property until Norman became sole owner of the farm decades later.

During my first meeting with Judge Norman Sortor, he told me he and his father, Fred, often ate lunch beneath a huge cottonwood on the farm.

"My father used to point his finger to where the *Arabia* lay hidden," Norman said. "He told me stories about the whiskey and the men who had tried to recover it."

Fred died when Norman was only nine. He never forgot the stories his father had told him, and he continued the tradition with his own family. Norman and his wife, Beulah, along with their children, Patricia, Edith, and Martha, often worked together harvesting hay from the farm. While taking a break and sipping lemonade under the giant cottonwood, Norman would retell the story of the *Arabia* and the cargo of whiskey.

I can just imagine the hardships the Sortors endured while working the farm: blisters rising on their hands, their feet aching from guiding and pushing the plow, eyes stinging from sweat on a scorching hot day, dust rising from the fields and choking them. The Sortors worked hard from dawn till dark, all the while wondering what treasures lay beneath them.

For every generation of Sortors, someone had tried to excavate the *Arabia*, but all had failed. Now, in the twilight of Norman's life, his dream of seeing the *Arabia* and her treasures was coming true.

Norman Sortor was independent and self-sufficient. Unfortunately, he was diagnosed with cancer prior to the excavation and was so weak he visited the dig only once. In his absence Norman's family would often come to the excavation to check on our progress. They reported back to him each day, sharing stories about the treasures aboard the *Arabia*, and showing him videos and pictures of our progress. One family member said, "In all the years I have known Norman, I feel closer to him now than ever before. His eyes light up when we talk together about the *Arabia*. For the first time in my life, I have something to offer Norman."

Although we found no barrels of whiskey, we did discover cases of cognac, and we immediately delivered a bottle to Norman. One week later, I called Beulah, Norman's wife, and asked if Norman had tasted the cognac.

"No," Beulah said, "I can't get him to try it, but he sure is admiring it."

When we decided to create a museum instead of selling our 85-percent share, we presented our plans to Norman and Beulah and asked them to consider how best to separate out their portion of the cargo.

The day we discussed the division of artifacts, we were all tense. We had become emotionally attached to our discoveries, and many pieces were one of a kind. We could not simply break off 15 percent of a glass lamp or tear a sleeve off an *Arabia* shirt.

Dad and Dave met with Norman and Beulah at their home. Norman's strength was quickly slipping away, but his mind remained strong.

"We have thought this over," Norman said, "and have decided the best thing for the *Arabia* artifacts is that they remain together, as one single collection. Therefore, we will choose only 25 artifacts to give to our children and grandchildren. We will select only items that there are multiples of, and nothing that will break up a set. The remainder of the artifacts you can keep for the museum."

A few weeks later, Norman passed away. When the funeral was over, Norman's family came back to his home for the traditional dinner. As the family gathered around the table, Beulah emerged from the back room with a tray of drinking glasses and the unopened bottle of *Arabia* cognac. They poured a sip of history for each person and toasted "Judge Norman Sortor," a fine, fine man, from either side of the bench.

Preservation and Museum Development

Our lives have forever changed since breaking ground above the *Arabia*. No longer treasure hunters, our choice to save the collection and establish a museum had created a sense of panic among our families. We returned to our full-time jobs and began making loan payments. This, combined with caring for the artifacts and creating a museum from scratch, left us little time to congratulate ourselves on excavating the *Arabia*.

Establishing a museum and preserving tons of artifacts is a difficult task, even for trained professionals. The list of requirements was depressingly long: (1) complete artifact stabilization; (2) learn preservation techniques and preserve thousands of artifacts in time to open the museum; (3) choose a location, and either construct a new building or renovate an existing structure; (4) design museum display cases; (5) arrange the artifacts with supporting graphics and written text; (6) create a film pertaining to the history of the *Arabia* and the excavation for the museum's theater presentation; (7) learn a business traditionally operated by historical academics with strong backgrounds in education; (8) keep it financially viable; and (9) keep our "day jobs" going. These tasks, and many others, weighed heavily upon us all. To succeed in this multifaceted endeavor, we all had to work diligently.

Completing the stabilization of the artifacts was of the highest priority. Family and many friends joined in the effort as we froze textiles and leathers, cleaned metals and stored them safely away, monitored artifact storage tanks, and inspected bottled goods daily.

An 80-foot long, 20-foot wide and eight-foot deep hole, which we dug and lined with a rubber liner, provided the temporary storage environment for our largest artifacts. We submerged the two prefabricated houses, stern, capstan, and supporting structure for one paddle wheel until the museum could receive them.

We completed artifact stabilization during the three months following the excavation and started on preservation.

Preservation was a huge challenge. We knew nothing about freshwater preservation, and we moved forward, equipped only with determination and desire.

I started the long journey toward conservator by picking up the phone and calling museums and universities throughout the United States. After several days and many hours on the phone, I had learned a

Excavators dug a large pool to hold the Arabia's *stern, support structure for the larboard paddle wheel, and two prefab houses. To help keep the artifacts stable and the water pure, a hose ran water into the pool continually until the museum received them, two years later.*
Photo by Bob Hawley

great deal. Unfortunately, very little of what I learned was about preservation.

Our families' desire to responsibly preserve the *Arabia* collection did little to endear us to most conservators. Our lack of proper credentials brought forth an abrupt gruffness from some professional conservators. Many seemed more interested in who was funding us, and what our background was. A conservator in the Great Lakes region shared this advice: "I'll be glad to help. Open up the excavation and bury everything you found aboard the *Arabia*. You and your associates have no business handling this collection."

With a knot of frustration in my stomach, my search for helpful conservators led me to Norway, Iceland, Germany, Sweden, and England. The Europeans were generous with their advice. My long-distance search eventually led me to conservators with the *Mary Rose Trust*, in Portsmouth, England.

Henry the VIII had built the *Mary Rose* as part of his naval expansion

Except for a broken handle, these rolling pins were identical in size and shape upon their discovery. It is easy to see the difference between the preserved rolling pin and the one that dried without treatment. **Photo by Greg Hawley**

program. It sank in 1545, in action with the French. Researchers spent nearly three decades, starting in the 1960s, studying, salvaging, and preserving the *Mary Rose* and her cargo. Although the *Mary Rose* sank in a salt water environment, preservation techniques for large timbers were similar. Conservators gave us invaluable advice on the stabilization and future preservation of the stern and larboard paddle wheel support.

They also suggested I contact the Canadian Conservation Institute (CCI) and the Historical Resource Conservation Branch of the Canadian Parks Service.

Nails found in wooden kegs solidified together after 132 years beneath the water. Separating and cleaning them is a toilsome task. **Photo by Greg Hawley**

Through letters and countless hours on the phone, conservators from both the Parks Service and CCI taught me the ways of freshwater preservation. They provided vital information on rust removal and protective coatings for metals, appropriate soaps and methods for cleaning textiles, procedures for the freeze-drying of woods and leathers, and proper handling and storage techniques for all artifacts.

We purchased freeze-drying equipment and chemicals, began practicing conservation techniques on scraps of *Arabia* wood and leather, broken pieces of metal, and bits of fabric. After spending many hours learning and perfecting this new trade, we began the enormous task of removing 200 tons of artifacts from stabilized storage and preserving them.

Cleaning and caring for the collection was critical to our success. But we needed a museum to profile the artifacts. After the news media reported our story, several local communities and area executives showed interest in the *Arabia* collection as a public attraction. We inspected

Expecting her third child, Karen Hawley and father-in-law Bob Hawley prepare to stabilize tin with archival lacquer.
Photo by Florence Hawley

vacant land, existing buildings, reviewed area tourism numbers, and negotiated lease agreements. We examined each potential museum site and decided that renovating an existing building was most economical.

There are only a few museums in the United States that are not subsidized. If the *Arabia* museum was to succeed, it too must function in the minority. Our families were not candidates for federal or state grants. If the museum failed to support itself financially, creditors could force us to sell the collection to satisfy debts. To succeed, contributions for museum development must come from our families in the form of old-fashioned hard work and sweat equity.

We based our decision to establish a for-profit museum on several factors. First, the likelihood of our families receiving grant funds without academic credentials or experience in museum operations was slight. Second, a not-for-profit museum requires a board of directors, and with so many decisions to make in a short time, a big committee controlling funds could result in disaster. Third, a number of historians

Greg Hawley places artifacts into a freeze-dryer for moisture removal.
Photo by Karen Hawley

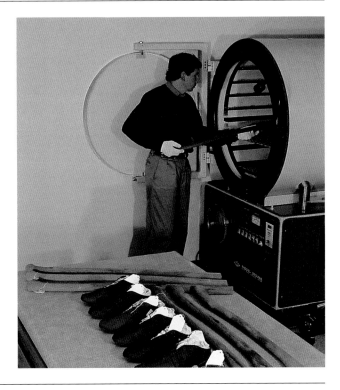

and museum professionals predicted our failure without expert help and community funding. Since nothing is more inspirational than a challenge, these negative remarks gave us ample motivation to succeed on our own merit.

After a great deal of deliberation, our families chose to establish the Arabia Steamboat Museum in Kansas City, Missouri, at the historic City Market. City founders established the City Market in 1857, just one year after the *Arabia* sank. Adjacent to the City Market and at the river's

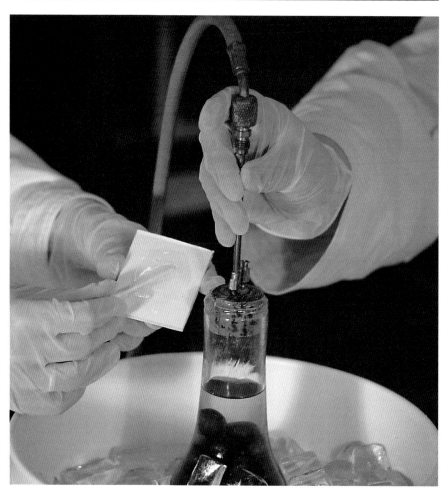

To maintain bottled fruits and vegetables, Bob Hawley developed a procedure to purge oxygen from the bottles using nitrogen. Photo by Greg Hawley

edge was Westport Landing, the *Arabia's* final stop before sinking ten miles upstream. From a historical standpoint, the City Market was an ideal location to establish the museum.

The City Market was in the middle of a face-lift when city officials approached us about the *Arabia* collection. Developers were renovating old buildings into loft apartments and revitalizing retail businesses in the area. They were looking for an attraction that would lure tourism to the City Market, and the *Arabia's* treasure seemed a perfect match. The building we selected had been a produce warehouse since the 1940s. The floors were slippery with dirt and grease. Walk-in coolers, long since abandoned, filled the basement. Crates containing rotting vegetables sat unattended in dark corners; and one very large, but very dead rat, added to the building's grimness.

Despite the filth and disarray, the building had virtue in its structural soundness and size. The building was nearly impervious to fire; and the walls, floors, and ceiling were built entirely of concrete. The ceiling height was adequate, and the building's size went well beyond the 40,000 square feet required for displaying and preserving the collection, as well as having space for offices, a gift shop, and a snack bar.

Due to the building's size and configuration, we agreed to lease the basement for the artifact exhibit and a portion of the upper space for the gift shop and snack bar.

The news of the Arabia Steamboat Museum reached the local newspapers and TV, and several museum professionals approached us with design proposals. Most of the experts suggested we educate the public by displaying very few artifacts and a lot of text. However, we wanted to reveal the frontier through large quantities of household goods, school supplies, international finery, and building necessities, not walls covered with printed material.

All of us and our wives traveled to different cities searching for ideas at other museums and tourism attractions. After our fact-finding trips, we met back in Independence to discuss our observations. Each museum we visited was different, but they all did have one thing in common: they were not profitable. Taxpayers or corporations subsidized their operations, a luxury not available to our families.

Dave built a model of the building out of one-quarter-inch foam board. The scale of the model was one inch to one foot, and when completed it stretched 20 feet across the basement of his home.

After dedicating thousands of hours to the museum design, the final features included the following: (1) a 100-seat theater featuring a 15-minute introductory film; (2) a display room showing artifacts from international origins, including perfume from France, trade beads from Italy, and dishware from England; (3) displays resembling an old town hosting thousands of items, including bottles, tinware, dishware, tools, food, liquor, rubber products, guns, and much more; (4) a textile and leather case showing a variety of coats, shirts, socks, hats, buttons, shoes, boots, bridles, saddles, and whips; (5) a hardware case displaying thousands of building supplies; (6) a preservation lab where visitors watch the cleaning of artifacts; (7) a full-scale replica of the *Arabia* main deck, complete with boilers, engines, and working paddle wheel.

The first year turned into the second. Preservation of the collection continued to go well, as did the museum design. We spent 40 to 50 hours each week at our regular jobs, and close to the same on the *Arabia* project. The grueling schedule was reminiscent of the dig, but without the adventure. My wife and kids continued to feel abandoned. After working on artifacts at the lab until midnight, I would come home to find my wife awake, and sewing up an old boot or cleaning a powder flask from the *Arabia*. "Don't do this to our family again," she often said, while continuing to sew or clean.

In January 1991, our families moved the stern, larboard paddle wheel support structure, steam engines, and boilers into the museum. Due to the enormous size of these objects, we had to set them into place before workers installed the museum's roof.

The stern and larboard paddle wheel support structure had remained underwater for two years to prevent deterioration from premature drying. Designed into the display of these large structures was equipment that would continually saturate the wood with strengthening chemicals. However, the equipment was not yet operational. To prevent deterioration, we soaked the wood daily before wrapping them with large sheets of plastics to prevent drying.

With the largest boat pieces in place, contractors installed the roof and worked on the interior. Because the city owned the building, union workers built and installed the walls, fire sprinkler systems, and the majority of the electrical components. Traditionally, unions object to non-union labor working on a building at the same time. However, union leaders granted us permission to work as a family on the job site, and we appreciated the cost-saving gesture. Each night, my family entered the museum and worked on audio, telephone, and security systems, ran electrical wires for display lighting, plumbing for preservation, and much more.

By July 1991, we completed most of the major construction. The intricate work of outfitting the gift shop and concession stand, writing text and installing photographs, building displays and placing thousands of artifacts within the museum finally began.

For the following four months, many of us worked 90 to 100 hours per week at the soon-to-be Arabia Steamboat Museum. It was exhausting work, but there was plenty of motivation. The total amount borrowed, combined with our personal investments and investor contributions, had reached $1,450,000. For several months, we had borrowed money from the bank just to pay the interest on the loan.

Lack of money was not the only reason we invested long hours in the *Arabia* project. My family life had totally disintegrated. My six-year-old son, Derek, asked my mom one day, "Is church on vacation, Grandma?"

When I heard this, my heart sank. I didn't think he'd noticed our lack of church attendance. On another occasion, my mother and I were discussing grandchildren when mom, with a tear in her eye, stated, "I've got eight grandchildren, Greg, and there is grass growing beneath the swing in my yard."

Five years earlier when this project began, hunting buried treasure seemed a quick way to riches. I had hoped the wealth provided by this venture would secure a host of tangible and otherwise unattainable things for my family. In reflection, it had cost my family dearly.

Despite the hardships, I believed a power greater than my own influenced the *Arabia* project. There had been too many narrow escapes, too many coincidences, and too much good fortune. I may never understand the Divine Will that influenced this project so profoundly, but I know the events that transpired transcend any earthly explanation.

The *Arabia* collection, once destined for the auction block, will give future generations both a window into the past and provide a testimony to God's work.

Late in the evening on November 12, 1991, we stood in the museum

The huge quantities of locks, nails, hinges, and other hardware illustrate the need for new construction on the frontier.   **Photo by Greg Hawley**

Displays featuring hundreds of bottles, dishes, platters, bowls, and pitchers represent a tragic loss for frontier merchants and passengers on the Arabia.   **Photo by Greg Hawley**

without the sound of hammers pounding or drills spinning. The following day marked the grand opening of the Arabia Steamboat Museum, and the anniversary of the ground breaking on the *Arabia* three years earlier. We had accomplished what many predicted impossible. Using unconventional methods of design and construction, we successfully established the Arabia Steamboat Museum without public or government funds.

Florence and Bob Hawley arrange fabic in the textile display. Exhibits showing silk from China, wool pants, red shirts, and sweaters, reveal the fashions of the frontier in 1856.
Photo by Greg Hawley

A time capsule is often used to describe the huge quantities of frontier supplies on display at the Arabia Steamboat Museum.
Photo by Greg Hawley

above *Attached to the Arabia's original engine and larboard support structure, a 28-foot reproduction of the steamers paddle wheel turns in a pool of water.*

right *Visitors from around the world come to see the treasures recovered from the steamboat* Arabia.

Photos by Greg Hawley

CHAPTER 13

The Arabia Museum

The Arabia Steamboat Museum opened to the public on November 13, 1991, with a formal ribbon-cutting ceremony. It was a festive yet tense occasion. I was not confident the museum would satisfy the crowd's expectations. With speeches completed, we stepped forward, and, as if in slow motion, cut the ribbon. The crowd cheered and the ribbon settled to the floor; the Arabia Steamboat Museum was open for business.

As visitors quietly entered into the collection area and strolled by thousands of displayed artifacts, I saw an emotional transformation take place in almost everyone. People began to liven up, mingling with one another and talking with increasing enthusiasm. In observing the crowd's reaction, I realized the *Arabia* collection and the story it told dissolved barriers between strangers.

"My mother ironed her clothes with an iron just like that one," one woman reminisced, pointing to the case.

"My grandfather had one of those," I heard a man mutter, as he gazed at a display of carpentry tools.

In the crowd was an elderly woman who quietly viewed each case. Near the museum exit, she approached me and asked if I had "saved the clothing."

"We sure did," I said. "And if you want, I'll take you back to the textile exhibit and show it to you."

"I don't mean the clothing you found on the steamer. I want to know if you saved the clothing you wore during the excavation?"

"I hadn't given it much thought," I said.

"After you're dead," she responded, "I'll want to see them on display."

"Wow," I thought to myself. "What a strange thing to say. This woman is twice my age, but seems confident she will outlive me. Does she know something I don't?" I wanted to respond by saying, "I'd rather see your clothes on display than mine."

Still, I realized what she meant. Saving the *Arabia* collection and sharing it with the community made us part of the story. Although it was flattering to hear a request for immortalization upon my death, I preferred the status quo.

I do not know how many hands I shook that day or how many hugs I received, but when the last visitor departed and we secured the doors, I felt relieved. Our visitors had fallen in love, as we had, with the *Arabia*.

Greg and his family continue to help operate the Treasures of the Steamboat Arabia Museum in Kansas City. It has become not only a tradition, but also a privilege to greet museum visitors and share stories of their adventure. From left, they are Derek, Megan, Karen, Greg and Kristin.   Photo by Tim Ross

That night after my family fell asleep, I entered the basement of my home and gathered up the clothing I had used to dig the *Arabia*: waders, rain gear, hat, goggles, and coat. Placing them in a plastic sack, I included a note for my children to read when I am gone. "These are the clothes I wore when I excavated the *Arabia*. This clothing, like the pioneers who traveled aboard the steamer, and the treasure found within, is part of the story. Please display them in the museum as my final contribution to the legend of the Great White *Arabia*.

AFTERTHOUGHTS

With the *Arabia* excavation completed and the museum open, I find myself wondering what treasures lie hidden aboard other steamboats. Perhaps it is better that I do not know. Each of us, including myself, needs a little mystery, wonderment, and hope to entertain and challenge our imagination. For some it is wishing on a shooting star, searching the grass for a four-leaf clover, or simply finding a lucky penny. For others it is contemplating what the family dog is dreaming about or looking skyward at the sound of migrating geese and wondering how they find their way.

My father often says that ignorance is bliss, and he is probably correct. There is high adventure in the unknown and along uncharted courses. If we knew the contents of a book before we read it, or what is beyond the summit of a mountain before we climb it, or what is aboard a sunken steamboat before we dig it, there would be no wonder, no mystery, no dreams in life. Whether we are digging for buried treasure or pondering the call of a whippoorwill at dawn, we should value the wonder of the unknown and the thrill of discovery.

Treasure hunting is a universal dream. For those who have pursued the fantasy of discovery, it is not without cost and sacrifice. The hypnotic trance delivered by images of gold and silver can consume your soul. It is a dangerous business that has the power to disrupt the commitment to God and family, the priority and essence of life. In reflection, I know this is true.

G.H.

GLOSSARY

Steamboating terms applying to the *Arabia*

BAR, SANDBAR: A riverbed obstruction of sand or gravel.

BOILER: An iron tank partially filled with water in which steam is generated by heat passing through internal ducts or flues.

BREAKS: An unusual rippling of the water caused by an obstruction hidden just beneath the surface of the river.

CAPSTAN: A hand-operated rotating cylinder on the stern area of the main deck, used as a winch for drawing rope lines.

CRANK: A metal shaft attached to the pitman and paddle wheel shaft, changing linear motion into circular motion.

DOCTOR, DOCTOR ENGINE: An auxiliary engine used to pump water into the boilers.

DRAFT: The depth to which the hull extends into the water.

HATCH: An opening in the hold through which cargo is passed.

HOLD: The space enclosed by the hull, generally for cargo.

HULL: The shell or main body of a vessel.

KEEL: A timber or plate running lengthwise along the center of the bottom of a ship.

LARBOARD: The left side of the steamboat, looking forward.

MAIN DECK: The first deck, upon which the boiler and engine are installed.

PADDLE WHEEL: A wheel fitted with paddles, planks or "buckets," that propels a steamboat.

PITMAN ARM: A rod connecting a vibrating element to a rotating one. Hence the rod connecting the steam engine piston with the paddle wheel crank.

ROWDY: Deckhand or one who does heavy unskilled labor.

RUDDER: The hinged fin or plate at the stern that governs the direction of a vessel's movement.

STARBOARD: The right side of the steamboat, looking forward.

STERN: The rear part of the hull to which the rudder is hinged.

STROKE: The distance traveled by the piston during one complete revolution of the wheel.

YAWL: A small boat towed or carried aboard steamboats.

APPENDIX

The Treasure

The following is a generalized inventory of the artifacts recovered from the steamboat *Arabia*. Due to the enormity of the collection many items remain stabilized in frozen or underwater storage and are not part of this inventory. The inventory will continue to grow in quantity and accuracy until preservation is completed. Estimated time for artifact completion is the year 2022.

Arabia Steamboat Artifact Inventory

Artifact	Material	Count
Boat Parts and Related Articles		
Anchor	Steel	1
Counter weight for boiler	Steel	2
Caisson used in 1897 excavation	Steel plate	1
Boiler	Steel plate	3
Doctor engine	Cast iron/steel	1
Wheel hub	Cast iron/steel	2
Engine, paddle wheel	Cast iron/steel	1
Boiler ash grate	Cast iron	2
Water pump (two man)	Cast iron	2
Water pump, single handle	Cast iron	1
Forge	Sheet-iron	1
Stern section of boat	White oak	1
Hand truck	Wood/steel	2
Paddle wheel support structure	Wood/steel	1
Boiler fire wood	Wood	1
Hose	Rubber	1
Gasket	Rubber	3
Coal	Coal	25 pounds
Trim	Brass	6

Building Components

Various parts to door latch	Iron	700
Door handle	Iron	377
Door lock	Iron	338
Door lock hardware	Iron	180
Shutter screw	Iron	40
Gate Lock	Cast iron	2
Door latch	Cast iron	8
Rope fastener	Cast iron	27
Staple	Cast iron	14
Doorknob plate (round)	Cast iron	203
Doorknob plate with attachment	Cast iron	122
Rope guide	Steel	27
Key, bit	Steel	366
Hinge	Steel	314
Bolt	Steel	85
Nail	Steel	1,000,000
Screw, wood	Steel	10,000
Coffin screw	Steel	60
Tumbler padlock	Steel/cast iron	81
Screw pulley	Steel/cast iron	36
Key, bit	Brass	248
Padlock	Brass	1
Latch Plate	Brass	2
Keyhole cover	Brass	19
Door lock	Brass	12
Cupboard catch	Brass	41
Curtain rod cap	Brass	18
Keyhole plate	Brass	1
Square lock	Brass	19
Keyhole plate	Brass, Steel	45
Dead bolt	Porcelain/brass	8
Doorknob attached to door lock	Ceramic/steel	1
Doorknob	Porcelain/brass	10
Nut, square	Wood	40
Window pane	Glass	700
Doorknob	Ceramic/steel	186

Doorknob	Ceramic	78

Building Material

Prefabricated house	Wood	2
Lumber	Wood	10 tons

Clothing Accessories

Suspender pull	Brass	57
Buckle	Brass	111
Hook and eye	Brass	1,250
Eyelet for shoe	Brass	100
Belt	Leather/brass	72
Button	Glass, Rubber, Wood, and Bone	34,939

Coin

Penny	Copper	1
Half dime	Silver	1
Dime	Silver	2

Communication

Traveling inkwell	Glass/wood	163
Slate board	Slate	50
Slate pencil	Slate	1000
Writing pen	Brass, Wood	220
Nib	Steel	2,000
Pencil	Wood	506
Ink, writing (bottle)	Glass	11
Book cover	Leather	25

Container

Can	Tin	230
Can with lid and spout	Tin	1
Canning jar lid	Tin	14
Cylinder	Tin	5
Fuel can with folding lid	Tin	1
Tea canister/painted	Tin	1

Square tin	Tin	1
Spice box	Tin	7
Pail with lid and handle	Tin	11
Pail with locking lid	Tin	2
Peach can/opened	Tin	1
Coffee tin/painted	Tin	1
Oval box	Tin	5
Oil can	Tin	4
Round tin/flat	Tin	4
Canister with tin lid	Tin	10
Scroll bottle	Glass	96
Bucket	Wood	74
Washtub	Wood	20
Cargo shipping box	Wood	5000
Cargo shipping barrel	Wood	100
Canning jar	Ceramic	18
Whiskey jug	Ceramic	6

Cutlery

Butcher knife	Steel/wood	188
Fighting knife	Steel/wood	3
Table knife	Steel/horn	616
Fork	Steel/horn	676
Spoon	Pewter, Brass, Tin	665

Fatality

| Mule | Bone | 1 |

Firearms and Supplies

Percussion boot pistol	Steel/wood	14
Ram rod	Steel	14
Bullet mold	Steel	14
Flintlock trade gun	Steel, Brass, Wood	48
Percussion double barrel shotgun	Steel, Brass, Wood	2
Percussion single barrel shotgun	Steel, Brass, Wood	1
Percussion single barrel rifle	Steel, Brass, Wood	1
Shot	Lead	500,000

Powder flask	Brass	31
Powder horn	Brass/horn	9
Percussion cap	Brass	1000

Food and Drink
Bottled Goods

Gin	Glass	13
Wine	Glass	1
Cider champagne	Glass	13
Cognac	Glass	77
Sherry	Glass	2
"Western Mills Spice Sauce"	Glass	20
Large pickle	Glass	23
Small pickle	Glass	6
Pickled relish	Glass	6
Ketchup	Glass	12
Apples	Glass	5
Gooseberries	Glass	9
Rhubarb	Glass	2
Cherries	Glass	36
Currants	Glass	8
Blackberries	Glass	2
Peppercorn	Glass	1

Kegs containing

Ale	Wood/steel	1
Spiced pigs feet	Wood/steel	2
Butter	Wood/steel	10
Cheese	Wood/steel	10
Lard	Wood/steel	8
Mackerel	Wood/steel	2

Tin cans

Sardines	Tin	48
Oysters	Tin	24

Boxes

Grapes	Wood	5 lb.
Fish	Wood	5 lb.
Peppercorn	Wood	10 lb.

Cloves	Wood	10 lb.
Coffee	Wood	15 lb.
Nuts and seeds	Wood	12 lb.
Icebox contents		
Ox	Bone	1
Pig	Bone	2

Food Processing

Bread pan	Tin	2
Bowl with strainer insert	Tin	5
Bottom of coffee grinder	Tin	19
Baking pan	Tin	50
Coffee pot	Tin	27
Cookie cutter	Tin	3
Cake pan	Tin	12
Fluted muffin tin	Tin	5
Fluted pie pan	Tin	2
Funnel	Tin	4
Ladle	Tin	1
Nutmeg grinder	Tin	1
Pie pan	Tin	3
Pan with handle	Tin	2
Round lid	Tin	17
Strainer w/handle	Tin	1
Shaker	Tin	13
Shaker/top	Tin	1
Scoop with handle	Tin	9
Tea kettle	Tin	2
Pan w/pouring lip and no handle	Tin	1
Wash basin with three feet	Tin	6
Pot with swing handle	Cast iron	10
Skillet with long handle	Cast iron	13
Griddle	Cast iron	2
Pot with three feet	Cast iron	2
Meat grinder	Cast iron	1
Griddle	Cast iron	3
Grain grinder	Cast iron	4

Kettle with lid, spout	Cast iron	2
Deep skillet w/handle, pouring lip	Cast iron	1
Stove	Cast iron	1
Stove base	Cast iron	12
Coffee mill wrench	Cast iron	25
Pot with flared rim	Cast iron	1
Pot with straight sides	Cast iron	1
Stove foot	Cast iron	26
Ladle	Coconut	12
Coffee grinder	Wood	42
Rolling pin	Wood	2
Coconut dipper	Wood/coconut	15
Meat grinder with handle	Cast iron/wood	1

Food Service

Caster set with shaker top	Glass	24
Salt dip	Glass	18
Small drinking glass	Glass	5
Syrup jug	Glass	19
Candy dish	Glass	1
Shot/whiskey glass clear	Glass	30
Cruet with stopper	Glass	4
Davenport, Friburg		
Bowl	Ironstone	2
Bowl and lid	Ironstone	2
Pitcher	Ironstone	2
Plate	Ironstone	14
Sauce dish	Ironstone	14
Saucer	Ironstone	9
Davenport white		
Bowl	Ironstone	1
Pitcher	Ironstone	1
Plate	Ironstone	11
Saucer	Ironstone	8
Davenport, Cyprus		
Washbowl	Ironstone	2
Pitcher	Ironstone	3

Davenport, Queensware		
Bowl/basin	Ironstone	17
Davenport, white		
Saucer	Ironstone	9
Pitcher	Ironstone	4
Davenport, Shell Edge Blue		
Platter	Ironstone	26
Bowl	Ironstone	11
Davenport, Shell Edge Blue		
Plate	Ironstone	69
Unmarked Shell Edge Blue		
Casserole/rectangular	Ironstone	11
J. Wedgwood		
Platter	Ironstone	2
Casserole	Ironstone	2
Casserole lid	Ironstone	4
Plate	Ironstone	52
Dish	Ironstone	18
C. Meigh & Son		
Pitcher	Ironstone	2
Bowl	Ironstone	6
Casserole	Ironstone	2
T. Goodfellow		
Saucer	Ironstone	8
Cup	Ironstone	5
Bowl	Ironstone	1
Unmarked, white		
Bowl	Ironstone	45
Unmarked White Dishes		
Plate	Ironstone	88
Cup	Ironstone	27
Container and lid	Ironstone	11
Pitcher	Ironstone	2
Lid	Ironstone	1
Bowl	Ironstone	9
J. Heath		
Pitcher	Ironstone China	2

Edwards & Hall, Felsphar, Opaque

Plate	China	9

J & R Booth

Platter	China	1

J. Edwards, Dale Hall, Felsphar Opaque

Bowl	China	11
Teapot	China	1
Sugar bowl	China	1
Pitcher	China	2
Shell shaped dish	China	2
Oval platter	China	4
Oval vegetable dish	China	4

Gold rimmed dishes

Dinner plate	China	2
Salad/pie plate	China	11
Sauce dish	China	10
Saucer	China	11
Sugar bowl	China	1
Tea pot	China	1

Imperial French

Saucer	China	2

Real Ironstone

Relish	China	2

Pankhurst & Co. Ironstone

Bowl	China	1

Unmarked Floral Tea Set

Teapot	China	1
Saucer	China	5
Cup	China	20

Unmarked brown/drip design

Pitcher	Ceramic	2

"...NET & BRO. PITTSBURGH"

Yellow ware bowl	Ceramic	5

Unmarked Yellow ware

Bowl	Ceramic	1
Syrup jug	Ceramic	1
Serving tray	Cast iron	13

Cup with handle	Tin	12
J & J Water Dale Hall Pottery		
Lonoport Raised relief pitcher	Porcelain	1

Footwear

Boot and shoe	Leather	5,000
Shoe	Rubber	252

Horse and Stable

Curry comb	Wood/steel	120
Riding whip	Willow	36
Bridle button ornament	Brass	4
Ring for harness or bridle	Brass	27
Bridle or harness rosette	Brass	5
Stirrup	Steel/brass	18
Spur	Steel/brass	19
Bridle	Leather	24
Bullwhip	Leather	24
Saddle	Leather	5
Rein	Leather	24
Bullwhip	Rubber	12
Bit	Steel	11

Household Accessories

Coat hook	Iron	239
Bootscraper	Iron	9
Bed caster	Iron	27
Bootjack	Iron	6
Steelyard scale	Steel	11
Bed caster	Steel	1
Lightning rod bracket	Steel	13
Curtain rod holder	Steel	18
Sash pulley	Steel	28
Bunghole gate valve	Steel	3
Animal trap	Steel	9
Bed spring	Spring steel	20
Curtain rod	Brass	24

Tray	Brass	12
Bar	Lead	1,040
Spigot	Pewter	43
Dust pan with no handle	Tin	1
Lacquered tray	Tin	12
Washboard	Wood/tin	4
Cuspidor	Ceramic	1
Statuette	Glass	2
Lightning rod insulator	Glass	14
Hemp rug	Hemp	1
Knob for door	Wood	48
Clothespin	Wood	418
Mirror and frame	Wood/glass	29

Indian Trade Goods

Bead	Glass, Silver, Brass	5,000,000
American vermilion	Paint	6 boxes

Jewelry

Earring, pairs	Gold plate	13
Brooch	Gold plate	41
Ring	Gold plate	10
Ring	Gold	6

Lighting Devices and Related Articles

Wall candle holder	Tin	1
Lamp/top	Tin	2
Lantern top with hanging ring	Tin	2
Lantern	Tin	6
Candle mold	Tin	6
Candle stick holder	Tin	24
Whale oil lamp	Glass, Tin, Brass	67
Match containers with matches	Wood	179
Candle	Tallow	3,168
Lamp	Brass	2
Lantern with glass globe	Steel/glass	4

Maintenance

Soap	Wood kegs/boxes	5
Clothes boiler top	Tin	1
Shoe polish	Tin	21
Sad iron	Cast iron	23
Clothes boiler	Tin/copper	2
Paint cans with paint	Tin	2
Clothes boiler bottom	Copper	8

Medicine and Related Articles

Unless otherwise noted name and contents of medicine unknown.

Pine Tar (keg)		6
"BARRELL'S INDIAN LINEAMENT"		3
"GENUINE ESSENCE"		1
"DR. D. JAYNES EXPECTORANT PHILADA."		1
"MEXICAN MUSTANG LINEAMENT"		8
"NERVE AND BONE LINEAMENT"		11
"MAGUIRE DRUGGIST ST. LOUIS MO"		9
Castor oil		24
Red liquid over clear		7
Pills in round tins		9
Lancet with three blades	Steel/brass	5
Lice comb	Bone	56
Bitters		
"OLD DR. J. TOWNSENDS"		1
"DR. J. HOSTETTER'S STOMACH BITTERS"		11
Leg bottle		11
Clear test tube shaped medicine bottle		
Dark amber liquid		30
Light amber		2
Light yellow		8
Light green		2
Medium brown		2
Cloudy		1
Clear		17
Empty		27
Yellow separated liquid		1

Cylinder shaped clear bottle   14

Multiple Use Artifact

Rope (3/8, 1/2 and 5/8 diameter)	Rope	1,000 feet
Chain	Steel	30
Hide	Leather	300

Musical Instruments

Jaw harp	Steel	48

Personal Gear

Umbrella	Wood	72
Pocket knife	Steel	328
Purse	Leather	25

Printing

Glue pot	Cast iron	2
Printers type	Lead	250,000
Printers block	Wood	1

Sawmill Equipment

Sawmill gear	Iron	6
Shaft	Iron	1
Lumber mill cog	Iron	2
Sawmill mill bearing	Steel	6
Sawmill blade round	Steel	2
Sawmill blade straight	Steel	6
Caster for moving logs	Steel	8
Belting	Leather	2

Sewing Equipment

Needle	Steel	5,000
Scissors	Steel	100
Thimble	Brass, Silver	469
Straight pin	Brass	10,000

Sewing Supplies

Bias tape	Wool	32
Rickrack	Wool	9
Empty spool	Wood	500
Yarn/skein	Wool	26
Yarn/ball	Wool	5
Embroidery floss	Silk	28
Thread	Silk	28
Thread twist	Silk	65

Sound Communication

Bell	Brass/bone	17
Cow bell	Steel	1

Textiles

Blanket	Wool	3
Mitten	Wool	16
Pants/men	Wool	9
Scarf	Wool	9
Shawl	Wool	1
Shirt	Wool	58
Sock	Wool	86
Underwear/long	Wool	35
Vest	Wool	10
Woman's sweater	Wool	1
Coat	Wool and beaver hair	103
Hat	Wool and beaver hair	247
Bolt	Wool, beaver hair and silk	60

Tobacco and Related Articles

Tobacco chew	Tobacco	200
Cigar	Tobacco	7,000
Cigar box	Wood	500
Keg of chewing tobacco	Wood	3
Pipe tobacco in lead foil	Lead foil/tobacco	100
Pipe stem	Bamboo	100
Pipe bowl	Clay	100

Toiletries

Hairbrush	Wood	51
Jar, cosmetic	Ironstone	24
Toothbrush	Horn	45
Hair pin	Steel	6,000
Eyeglasses	Brass/glass	24
Tinted eye protector	Leather/glass	24
Bonnet stick pin	Brass/glass	102
Mirror, hand held	Glass	42
Lotion with coconut scent	Glass	18
Lotion, unscented	Glass	32
Perfume	Glass	23
Perfume vial	Glass	4
Jar, cosmetic	Glass	11
Razor, straight	Steel	50
Chamber pot	Ironstone	1
Brush, shaving	Horn/hair	36
Hair pin	Rubber	13
Comb, tuck	Rubber	132

Tools

Auger handle	Wood	19
Ax handle	Wood	76
Ax head	Wood	235
Freight carrier	Wood	1
Tool box	Wood	1
Shovel handle	Wood	8
Scribe	Wood	12
Yardstick	Wood	3
Folding ruler	Wood	3
Hand ax	Wood	9
Saw handle	Wood	63
Saw brace	Wood	15
Pick handle	Wood	26
Hand maul	Wood	1
Wood screw	Wood	2
Wood vice	Wood	3

Wood nut	Wood	3
Shoe form	Wood	2
Mallet	Wood	1
Carpenter plane	Wood	50
Paint brush	Wood	10
Level	Wood	10
Hatchet with hammer	Wood/steel	11
Hatchet with claw	Wood/steel	2
Chisels with handle	Wood/steel	22
Eye auger with handle	Wood/steel	5
Leather punch	Wood/steel	3
T-Auger	Wood/steel	21
Saw set	Wood/steel	15
Block and tackle	Wood/steel	2
Screwdriver	Wood/steel	5
Hammer	Wood/steel	1
Square trowel	Wood/steel	3
Triangular trowel	Wood/steel	4
Draw knife	Wood/steel	25
File	Wood/steel	324
Hand saw and blade	Wood/steel	111
Spoke shave	Wood/steel	2
Snatch block	Wood/steel	2
Shovel	Wood/steel	20
Wrench	Iron	96
Block plane blade	Iron	8
Engine drain valve wrench	Iron	1
Barrel lifting tong	Iron	6
Cargo hook	Iron	6
Fireplace shovel	Iron	34
Fireplace tong	Iron	34
Bed key	Iron	19
Boiler tool	Iron	7
Needle nose pliers	Iron	3
Horse-shoe pliers	Iron	1
Carpenter adze	Iron	1
Poll adze	Iron	1

Gutter adze	Iron	1
Ship builder adze	Iron	1
Divider	Iron	12
Compass	Iron	2
Grub mattock	Iron	12
Fro	Iron	1
Pick	Iron	24
Hammer head	Iron	3
Gouge	Iron	9
Combination 5-hole wrench	Iron	30
Three-hole wrench	Iron	6
Crosscut saw	Steel	17
Chisel	Steel	35
Square	Steel	49
Swedge	Steel	16
Broad ax	Steel	9
Brace with bit	Steel	9
Gimlet	Steel	89
Keyhole saw	Steel	27
Drill bit	Steel	119
Pitch fork	Steel	3
Screw wrench	Steel	12
Tap and die set	Steel/iron	12
Sharpening stone	Sandstone	169
Tape measure	Tin/brass	6
Ladle with pouring edge	Cast iron	1

Toys

Charlotte doll	Porcelain	
Toy rickshaw	Tin	1
Marble	Clay, China	7
Doll arms and legs	Wood	80
Doll shoe	Leather	1
Sea shell	Shell	2

Wagon Parts

Wagon wheel	Wood/steel	6

Wagon axle	Wood/steel	2
Double tree	Wood/steel	1
Wagon tongue	Wood/steel	1

Weight Scales and Related Articles

Balance scale	Brass/steel	19
Spring scale	Brass/steel	12
Scoop for balance scale	Tin	5
Counterweights for steelyard scale	Iron	18
Steelyard scale	Steel	11

*Pioneers traded a wide range of goods with Native Americans. Beads and vermilion were items commonly used for trade, but other cargo discovered aboard the *Arabia* would have also qualified for barter.

Merchants Who Lost

On September 11, 1856, the *Daily Missouri Democrat* published a list of merchants that lost freight aboard the *Arabia*.

St. Joseph

Kay & Baily ....1 box merchandise
Donnell & Saxton ....8 boxes merchandise
J. H. Cook...3 boxes merchandise
Thomas Conneley ....3 boxes merchandise

Savannah

E. & Y. Impey & Co. .... 227 packages

Browsby Landing

R. Zimmerman & Co.................................1 sawmill and fixtures

Iowa Point

G. W. Brown ....10 bbls whiskey
McAllister, Orace & Co. ....7 packages
Baines, Strickland & Co. ....4 packages

St. Stephens

John O Knoll...2 packages
H. D. Kirk ....1 package

Hemmes Landing

Hawk & Dillion ....1 package

Linden

Tootle & Armstrong ....55 packages
Smith, Brown & McAlister ....9 packages
Steamer Ben Bolt......................................1 cook stove

Nebraska City

Hall & Baker ....1 bbl ale
C. Seigel ....11 packages

J. Garside ....11 packages

Glenwood
Tootle & Green ....30 packages

Bellevue
Allen ....11 packages
Sarpy & Kippy...3 packages
L. M. Peckham ....1 package
B. Lovejoy ....2 packages

Council Bluffs
F. M. Boyer ....1 package
Stutsman & Donnell ....55 packages
Thompson & Butts ....15 packages
M. Rogers ....13 packages
Cassady & Test ....1 package
Babbitt & Robinson ....4 packages
C. Gore ....2 packages
Keys & Co. ....54 packages
J. R. Washington ....20 packages
Tootle & Jackson ....106 packages
Geo. Doughty & Co....................................21 packages

Omaha
J. Jones ....22 packages
O. B. Smith ....9 packages
Tootle & Jackson ....5 packages
H. W. Richmond.......................................1 package
A. Sheldon..1 package
Schneider & Hardford..............................4 packages
W. Shirids ....6 packages
M. Handon ....28 packages
Armstrong & Clark ....357 packages
Stutesman & Donnel.................................202 packages
Willimson & Roach...................................5 packages

Florence
L. Keiler..20,000 feet lumber

Blackbird Hill
Blackbird Mission ....29 packages

Sioux City
Burnes, Roberts & Co. ....100 packages
D. O. Shea...3 packages

Logan
Tracy & Papin ....720 packages
Tracy & Papin ....2 houses
J. Harri ....20 packages

The Ballad Of Young Charlotte
By William Lorenzo Carter

Fair Charlotte lived by the mountain side
In a wild and lonely spot,
No dwelling was for three mile around
Beside her father's cot.

And yet on many a wintry night,
Young swains would gather there,
Her father kept a social board,
For she was very fair.

Her father loved to see her dress
Gay as a city belle,
She was the only child he had,
And he loved his daughter well.

It was New Year's night, the sun was down,
Why look her anxious eye,
So off from the cottage window forth,
As the evening shades drew night?

At a village inn, fifteen miles off,
Was a merry ball that night,
The winds without were as cold as death,
But her heart was warm and light.

How brightly beamed her laughing eye
As the well-known sound she heard,
When driving up to the cottage door
Young Charlie's sleigh appeared.

"O daughter dear," her mother said,
"This blanket round you fold,
It is a dreadful night without,
And you'll catch a fatal cold."

"Oh, no, no, no," fair Charlotte said.
And she laughed like a gypsy queen,
"To ride in blankets muffled up,
I never can be seen."

"My silken cloak is quite enough,
You know, it's lined throughout,
Besides, I have a silken shawl,
To tie my neck about."

Her bonnet and her shawl were on,
She stepped into the sleigh,
And away they ride by the mountain side,
And over the hills away.

There's life in the sound of the merry bells,
As over the hills they go,
What a creaking noise the runners make,
As they bite the frozen snow.

Along the bleak and dreary way
Five lonely miles they passed,
When Charles in a few and frozen words
The silence broke at last.

"Such a night as this I never knew,
The reins I scarce can hold,"
Fair Charlotte said in a feeble voice,
"I'm exceedingly cold."

He cracked his whip and urged his team
More swiftly than before,
Until five other lonely miles
In silence they passed o'er.

"How fast," said Charles, "the freezing ice
Is gathering on my brows,"
Fair Charlotte said in a feeble voice,
"I'm getting warmer now."

Away they ride through the frozen air
In the glittering starry light,
Until at length the village inn
And the ballroom was in sight.

They reached the door, young Charles stepped out
And held his hand to her,
"Why sit you there like a monument
That hath no power to stir?"

He called her once, he called her twice,
She uttered not a word,
He held his hand again to her,
But still she never stirred.

He took her hand within his own,
It was cold and like a stone,
He tore the veil from off her face,
The moonlight on it shone.

Then swiftly through the lighted hall
Her lifeless form he bore,
Fair Charlotte was a stiffened corpse,
And words spake nevermore.

He sat himself down by her side and
the bitter tears did flow,
And he said "My young intended bride,
I never more shall know."

He threw his arms around her neck
and kissed her marble brow,
And his thoughts went back to where she said,
"I'm getting warmer now."

He bore out into the sleigh
and with her he drove home,
And when he reached the cottage door,
O how her parents mourned.

They mourned the loss of their daughter dear
while Charles mourned o'er their gloom,
Until with grief his heart did break,
and they slumber in one tomb…

SELECTED BIBLIOGRAPHY

Eleanor, George. *The Dolls of Yesterday*. New York: Bonanza Books, 1948.

Finch, Ralph. "The Mystery behind the G-IXs." *Souvenir Program of the Federation of Historical ottle Collectors Expo*. Toledo, Ohio, 1992.

Folkwear. "Patterns from Times Past." San Rafael, CA.

Hanson, Charles E., Jr. *The Northwest Gun*. Nebraska State Historical Society, Publication in Anthropology, No. 2, Lincoln, NE, 1956.

——."A Paper of Vermilion." *The Museum of the Fur Trade Quarterly*. Vol. VII, No. 3, Museum of the Fur Trade, Fall 1971.

Harris, Elizabeth. *A Bead Primer*. The Bead Museum, Prescott, AZ 1987.

Henrywood, R. K. *Relief-Molded Jugs* 1820-1900. Printed in England by the Antique Collectors Club, 5 Church St., Woodbridge, SuHolk, Edition 1984.

Hunter, Louis C. *Steamboats on the Western Rivers*. Dover Publication, Inc. 1993. p. 429.

Ingalls, John James. *Ingalls Collection*. Manuscript Collection at the Kansas State Historical Society, Topeka, KS,1858.

Missouri State Archives. *Johnston Verses Steamboat Arabia*. Jefferson City, Missouri, March 24, 1856.

Kansas City Star. "The Legend Of The Lost Arabia And Its Treasure Exploded." June 1910.

Marks, C. R. *Annals of Iowa*. Vol. VII, No. 5, Des Moines, IA., 3rd Series, Monona County, Iowa, Mormons, April 1906.

Merrick, George B. *Steamboats and Steamboatmen of the Upper Mississippi*. Burlington, IA: Saturday Evening Post, 1913 - 1920.

Mulligan, Adair. "Straining Up a Cord Bed." *Country Living*, Dover Publishing Inc., Mineola, New York, May 1993.

Record Group 94, Office of Adjutant General, Regular Army Muster Rolls and Returns, U.S. 2nd Infanty Staff. *Muster Roll of the Field, Staff, and Band of the Second Regiment*, August 10, 1855.

Twain, Mark. *Life on the Mississippi*. Penguin Group, New York, NY, 1961.

Smith, Patricia R., Bill Schroder. *Antique Collector's Dolls*, series 1 and series 2. Collector's Books, Puducah, Kentucky, 1975.

Twain, Mark. *Following the Equator, A Journey Around the World*. New York and London, Harper and Brother, 1899.

———. *Which Was the Dream? And Other Symbolic Writings of the Later Years*. Edited with an introduction by John S. Tuckey. Berkeley: University of California Press, 1967.

Williams, Peter. *Wedgwood: A Collectors Guide*. Radnor, PA, Wallace - Homestead, 1992.

Woodward, Arthur. *Indian Trade Goods*. Oregon Archaeological Society. Binford and Mort, Portland, Oregon, 1965.

For information about
the Arabia Steamboat Museum,
related books, videos,
and artifact reproductions call or write to:

Arabia Steamboat Museum
400 Grand Blvd.
Kansas City, Missouri 64106
Office (816) 471-1856
Fax (816) 471-1616

Visit us on the World Wide Web
at www.1856.com